EARL OF OAKHURST

MADELINE MARTIN

PROLOGUE

L ochslin Castle, Scotland
October 1819

JAMES MACKENZIE KNEW HOW MANY OUNCES OF WHISKY would fit in the false bottom of a carriage. He knew the best path from Scotland through England to avoid the Runners and the exact place on a man's head to hit to make him drop like a stone. He even knew how many glasses of whisky it took to make him lose his senses. Eight. And every time he swore it'd never happen again.

What he did not know, however, was how to be an earl. Or at least nothing beyond what was required of a valet.

According to the letter in MacKenzie's hand, he would now require such instruction, as he was the very improbable, and quite unprepared, Earl of Oakhurst.

Rich laughter rose up from the overstuffed chair by the fireplace where MacKenzie's friend, Alistair, the Earl of Benton, raised a glass in mock salute to MacKenzie. "To the Earl of Oakhurst."

Alistair's mother, Madge, threw her wiry red hair over her skinny shoulder. "Losin' another fine Scotsman to the likes of England." She splashed more whisky into her glass and quit the room with a muttered string of curses.

MacKenzie watched her leave and continued to stare at the closed door as his mind reeled with the news he'd been dealt that morning. "I dinna know the first thing about being an earl."

Alistair scoffed and tossed the remnants of his whisky down his throat. Firelight caught the cut crystal glass and set it to twinkling. "Ye know more than ye think. The hardest thing about it is —" he put up one finger "—debutantes." Then another finger lifted. "And having to let a valet do every bloody thing for ye."

MacKenzie, who had spent the last five years as Alistair's valet, smirked at his former employer. "Ye'll be someone else's problem, going forward."

"I willna need a valet here in Scotland." Alistair got to his feet and poured himself an additional finger of whisky. "I only regret I willna be joining ye in London to reintroduce ye to society. No' with Emma so close to the babe's birth." The cocky grin on his face broadened to one of genuine joy at the expectation of his second child.

MacKenzie indicated the letter in his hand. "My grandmother is quite willing to accompany me."

It had been far too long since he'd seen her. Seven years, at least. When his uncle had died of an apoplexy and the earldom was left to his son, Gilbert—the arrogant popinjay—and the woman MacKenzie had been courting transferred her affections to the new earl. MacKenzie had fled to the Scottish estate he'd inherited from his mother to reunite with her family, which was where he'd stumbled upon Alistair.

They'd been fast friends, the two of them, both with Scottish blood that clashed with English roots. Both trying to outrun their English titles that might one day catch up with them. MacKenzie had considered himself fortunate to have escaped his title, especially when Alistair was snagged so early on.

It appeared MacKenzie's luck had not held.

The letter didn't mention how Gilbert had met his demise, but MacKenzie wouldn't be surprised to learn it had something to do with too much drink or a whore or a fight, or any combination of the three.

"Lord Kendal will be there to assist ye with navigating the ton." Alistair lifted the lid of a small wooden box on his desk. "He's no' working with whisky runners anymore, but I'm certain he's got some new scheme up his sleeve by now." Alistair approached MacKenzie and held out a small gold object.

MacKenzie took it, examining the "W" pin. The symbol of a member of the Wicked Earls' Club, London's most exclusive gentleman's club for earls, where the wickedest the ton had to offer, gathered. Rakes and rogues, scoundrels and smugglers, gamblers and fighters and every sort in between.

Alistair clapped a hand on MacKenzie's shoulder. "They'll welcome ye with open arms."

MacKenzie held the pin in the palm of his hand, still extended toward Alistair. "What about ye?"

"Alistair." A woman's soft voice came from the other side of the door, accompanied by the clicking of paws of their golden-haired dog, Beast. "Are you two still in there?"

The grin on Alistair's face widened. "I dinna need the pin anymore."

The door opened and a woman with brown hair entered the room. She was proceeded by a very large, very round belly and a bounding Beast who propelled himself into Alistair's legs, nearly knocking him over.

"Good evening, Lady Benton." MacKenzie offered a courteous bow.

She laughed and curtseyed as well as she could in such a delicate state. "Good evening, Lord Oakhurst. If you'll excuse me, I'll be taking my husband back now."

"Of course, my lady." MacKenzie bowed again. The way a valet did when given instructions.

Alistair chuckled and shook his head at MacKenzie. "It would appear the hardest part for ye may no' be letting a valet do everything for ye, but no' being a valet yerself."

MacKenzie scowled at his old friend, which only made Alistair chuckle harder. The Earl of Benton swept toward his countess with Beast trotting behind him, and together they quit the library, leaving MacKenzie alone with his misgivings about his new title.

It had taken over four months for the solicitors to find him, as he'd lost touch with his family over the years. Most likely they had learned of his position as Alistair's valet and traced him to Lochslin Castle. The ton would have opinions about his time as a valet. He knew he'd hear of it. As if they already didn't shun him for his brogue.

A wave of dread washed over him. He'd be returning to England. As an earl, to face everything an earl dealt with. The very things and people he'd run away from seven years ago.

❧ I ❧

London, England
November 1819

If one imagined the journey from Scotland to England on the edge of winter would take a considerable amount of time, one would be horribly and completely wrong. The sun had shone with excessive cheeriness and the horses had raced over the dry roads as effortlessly as Helios's chariot once flew through the open sky.

MacKenzie was in London. More specifically at Oakhurst Place, the four-story cream-colored stucco townhouse that sat behind an ornately erected wrought iron fence. Imposing white columns of the Corinthian order framed either side of the narrow structure. His grandfather had insisted on the bit of Grecian history being incorporated into the home and MacKenzie's grandmother had readily agreed.

MacKenzie's trepidation softened. He was woefully lacking in what was expected of him, but he had always held great affection for the Dowager Countess of Oakhurst.

His Hessians clicked up the walkway as the door opened to reveal a rather handsome butler with a head of thick black hair touched with silver at the temples.

"Welcome, my lord." The butler inclined his large, square-shaped jaw. "Lady Oakhurst has been expecting you." The man might look like a prize-fighting bruiser, but he sounded as regal as any proper butler.

MacKenzie strode into the vast entryway where the click of his boots turned into echoed clops upon the glossy marble flooring, and was promptly led up the stairs to the drawing room. The double doors flew open before he even reached the landing, and his grandmother burst through.

She was shorter than he remembered, her face lined more by age. Her fingers seemed as fragile as birds' bones where they gripped an ivory cane. Suddenly, the seven years of absence wrenched at his chest.

She had been the one who had coddled him as a boy after his mother's death, when he'd first been forced to move to England. His grandmother had fussed over his scraped knees and pressed kisses to his hot brow when he was burning with fever and held him as his heart broke with loss for his mum.

And he had repaid her by leaving her to grow old and frail alone.

"James." Tears filled her eyes and she hobbled forward, her weight heavy upon her cane. "My sweet James. You've come home at last." Her accent was as crisp as it'd ever been, her voice strong despite her delicate appearance.

"Ye needn't trouble yerself coming to me." MacKenzie rushed to her side in two great strides, settling an arm under hers to lead her back into the drawing room.

She leaned her scant weight on him and did not protest his aid. "George usually sees to me when I overexert myself." She glanced back at the butler with a smile. "Don't you, George?"

"Of course, my lady." The butler inclined his head.

"He does take good care of me." She allowed MacKenzie to assist her into the large seat. Her lavender gown spread elegantly on either side of her as she settled into the plush seat, the color indicative of her state of half mourning.

MacKenzie took the seat opposite her and regarded her with scrutiny. She looked stronger by the daylight streaming in through the large drawing room window. Her cheeks were flushed with excitement and her blue eyes bright. Her hair was the same steely gray beneath her lace cap that was trimmed with an excessive amount of ruffles.

The door closed as the butler left to instruct a maid to bring them tea.

"I've been gone too long," MacKenzie began.

His grandmother settled her small hand on his, those frail fingers weighing nearly nothing. She shook her head. "You needn't explain. You are a young man who needed to see to his own affairs. No one expected Gilbert would...well..." She tilted her head in place of speaking. "You're here now and that is all that matters."

"How did he...?" MacKenzie stopped the question before he could complete it.

Lady Oakhurst withdrew her cool, dry hand and sighed so greatly that her small shoulders rose dramatically. "It would appear he drowned in the Serpentine."

MacKenzie nodded solemnly and swallowed his rising curiosity, out of consideration for his grandmother.

She slid him a knowing look. "He was in his cups, of course," she continued unabashedly. "As was the..." She rolled her eyes. "...female companion he was with."

MacKenzie winced. How accurate his initial presumption of his cousin's death had been.

"It was quite the scandal." She lifted her chin with the same unflappable pride he'd always known her to possess.

Unsure what more to say, MacKenzie glanced around the

drawing room. It was exactly as he recalled from his boyhood. The silk-lined walls were the same pale blue, the polished dark wood furnishings laden with enough ornamental notions that he'd never been able to tell if they were new or old. Doubtless, it was safe to presume the latter.

What of Lady Judith? He bit back the inquiry. He shouldn't care about his cousin's fiancée, who had been strung on for years. Especially not when she'd abandoned MacKenzie's side for that of Gilbert's when he inherited the earldom.

"I dinna know how to be an earl," he said instead. "I never imagined it would fall to me."

"Surely, you learned something useful in your time as a valet." Lady Oakhurst raised her thin, gray brows at him.

The maid entered the room before MacKenzie could reply. She moved between them as discreetly as was possible, setting the teacups out, along with a pot and several biscuits.

"As I said, I dinna anticipate becoming an earl." It was a flimsy excuse, but all he had. The reasons why he had left were buried too deep to dredge up now. "I thought I could live my life without the earldom hovering over me."

"The ton will not be forgiving of your former life, but you already know that." Lady Oakhurst lifted the teapot with steady hands and filled MacKenzie's cup. "In regard to the earldom, I can teach you what you need to know." She attended to her own cup next and gracefully dropped in two lumps of sugar with pinched silver tongs.

"I'll be the most well-instructed earl in all of London." MacKenzie held his teacup tight with his fingertips, lest he drop the dainty thing.

"Flattery will get you everywhere, my dear James." She lifted her cup. "You always were such the silver-tongued devil." She shifted in her seat slightly and her face crumpled in pain. The teacup trembled in her hands, but through her characteristic iron will alone, she did not let the fragile porcelain loose.

MacKenzie leapt to his feet and pulled the teacup from her fingers. "What is it, Gemma?"

"This gout." She pulled her hem aside to reveal one bare foot, the side of which was swollen with inflammation. "It's so wretchedly painful, I cannot bear the slightest brush of anything against it." She waved her hand dismissively and smiled up at him. "You've not called me Gemma for years. I like it and would prefer you continue to do so."

"Of course, Gemma." He slowly returned to his seat, his muscles tense to come to her side again, should she require his aid.

"Have ye summoned a physician?" MacKenzie continued to stare at the floor where her swollen foot was hidden beneath a swath of lavender silk.

She nodded. "They tell me to limit my sherry and all the delicacies I enjoy. I think the pain of it is worth enduring when I consider what I must give up. But it's nothing I wish to speak on now. I'd prefer to discuss your first task as earl."

There was a solemn note to her tone, which made a little ball of ice form in the pit of MacKenzie's gut. "And that would be...?"

"Marriage."

He groaned into his cup of tea.

"I heard that," Gemma chastened. "At least you need not seek out another eligible lady if you prefer. Your cousin left behind a betrothed I find to be quite suitable. One you know rather well, I believe." She watched him carefully.

He lowered the teacup and shook his head in an attempt to stop her, even as the words tumbled from her lips. "Lady Judith Eaton."

The name alone jabbed deep into his chest, into a scar he'd thought long since healed over. Judith Eaton, the eldest daughter of Lord Chatsmore. The woman who had announced her betrothal to his cousin and who had broken MacKenzie's heart.

"I'll no' do it." MacKenzie shook his head more emphatically.

Gemma cast him a sympathetic look. "Her father anticipates you will be seeking her hand soon, to take the place of your cousin. Especially after a seven-year engagement. To avoid offending their family, I would recommend finding another betrothed. And with considerable haste."

LADY PENELOPE KEATS, ELDEST DAUGHTER OF THE EARL OF Bursbury, had always done everything asked of her, everything expected of her, with one glaring exception. She had not wed.

The subject was a sore one, which was pressed and prodded at often by nearly every person in Penelope's life. Not that she cared a whit about anyone's judgment. How could she, when lives were at stake?

Or at least their feet, in this particular case.

She gingerly held the man's foot as she examined the area to the left of his largest toe. The skin there was shiny and pink with inflammation.

"It does appear to be gout," Penelope said.

The man shifted uncomfortably in the chair he sat upon, setting the wooden legs creaking in protest beneath his corpulent form. "Is there a man about?"

Irritation prickled up Penelope's spine. After three years of offering her voluntary aid to the staff of St. Thomas's Hospital, it ought not to bother her anymore. And yet it did. Very much so.

She swallowed her ire and continued, "I assure you, I'm quite skilled in the area of—"

"I've been here before and the men have me patched up within a week."

Penelope offered a patient smile. "Your affliction in its very nature will clear within seven days' time, but it will come back if you do not address—"

"If I wanted a good nagging from a woman, I'd be home with

my wife." The man wheezed a laugh. "Be a good girl and fetch me a proper surgeon."

Penelope stood stiffly and swept from the room. No doubt she would think of just the right retort later that night while she was drifting off to sleep. Certainly, nothing came to her affronted tongue at the moment.

It was not the first time she'd encountered a patient who refused to allow her to see to them. She pushed through the door to her far right and entered the hospital room in search of a surgeon.

Dr. Bailey, the physician on staff at St. Thomas's, stood over a patient with something white in his hands. Whatever it was, he appeared to be lowering it onto the person's head.

He glared. "Leave, Lady Penelope."

"What are you doing?" She came deeper into the room and peered at the pale face beneath the mask-looking item.

"I'm seeing to a patient," he said through gritted teeth. "Get out now."

"But I—"

"In the hall now," he growled. "I want a word with you and not in front of this patient."

Dr. Bailey was a tall, lean man with a bit of white hair combed over his glossy pate like fine cotton, but he still cut an imposing figure when he glared down at Penelope, exactly as he did now.

"Lady Penelope, I will not have you questioning me." Dr. Bailey's lips were thin and folded together when he was annoyed, making him resemble something of a turtle. "Especially not in front of a patient."

Penelope had dealt with worse than an annoyed, pretentious physician in her time at St. Thomas's. She squared her shoulders, armed with the conviction of her medical knowledge. "It's only that I've never seen a treatment such as that. I—"

"That is enough," Dr. Bailey said crisply.

Penelope continued on as if he had not spoken. "The patient did not appear to be moving—"

"You do not know what you think you do." Dr. Bailey's eyes narrowed. "You are nothing more than a woman with wild ideas, who has been overly indulged."

"Those 'wild ideas' you refer to are derived from extensive research and observation," Penelope countered. "I deserve to be here as well as you or any other man."

She had gone too far. She knew she had. And she had no regret. Not one iota.

His turtle lips snapped tight together and he glowered at her hard before speaking. "I have tried to patiently tolerate your presence in this hospital in the years you have been meddling, but I will not allow it any longer." He did not move as a nurse rushed around him, her apron spotted with blood. Nor did he lower his voice. He wanted all to hear him.

"You are a debutante who has been allowed to play at a game you have no business in," he continued. "Furthermore, it is wildly inappropriate for a lady of your unfortunate marital status to be roaming about the hospital, unchaperoned."

Penelope folded her arms over her chest. "My unfortunate marital status?"

"You are unwed," he said simply. "You will never have a modicum of respect, or even a place here, until you are properly married."

Her heartbeat whooshed in her ears. Having her removed from volunteering at hospital had been an idle threat Dr. Bailey had insinuated in the past when Dr. Firth had been there to offer her his support. But Dr. Firth had relocated to Edinburgh six months ago, and Penelope was left without anyone to speak for her.

"What are you saying?" Penelope's stomach quivered even as she asked the question she already knew the answer to.

"I will be speaking with Dr. Astley Paston Cooper to have you removed from here." He offered a cold smile as he mentioned the President and Founder of the Medical and Chirurgical Society of London. "For your own protection, of course. As an unwed woman."

Tears burned in her eyes. Damn it. She would not cry now. Not in front of so awful a man. Not when she knew seeing her cry would make him gleefully satisfied.

She balled her hands into fists and did not stop squeezing until the edges of her fingernails nipped into her palms. She tilted her chin up defiantly. "I will continue to come until I am told otherwise."

"Then you can expect notice from Dr. Cooper within the week." Dr. Bailey offered a small bow, more mocking than respectful. "I saw your mother downstairs. I presume she's waiting for you. Good day, Lady Penelope."

Penelope swallowed down her ire and let it burn inside her churning stomach. Dr. Bailey knew well she did not wish to wed. Everyone at St. Thomas's knew as much. Her sole purpose in life was the pursuit of medical knowledge. She did not want a meddling husband controlling her, spending her dowry on drink and gambling even as he weighted her down with household responsibilities and children.

Penelope waited until Dr. Bailey returned to his patient before making her way downstairs to her mother. While Lady Bursbury was not pleased with Penelope's decision to forego marriage in pursuit of a life of learning, she had always been supportive in any way she could. Like meeting Penelope with the carriage each evening.

Penelope's mother waited in the main hall of the hospital. She was immaculately dressed, as one would expect from a countess. Her blue redingote was buttoned up against the stiff breeze carrying in the coming winter chill and a black bonnet covered her frosted auburn hair.

Her face brightened when she saw Penelope. "I believe that is the fastest you've come down yet." The smile on her face wilted at once. "Something is amiss. What is it?"

Penelope shook her head and did not speak until they were secured within the privacy of the carriage. "I spoke against Dr. Bailey today."

"Good," Lady Bursbury declared. "The buffoon deserves it and more. Your father will be proud of you for standing up for yourself."

"He says it is improper of me to be volunteering at the hospital and will petition Dr. Cooper to have me removed." Even now the weight of his words crushed in on Penelope's chest.

Lady Bursbury sat forward in her seat, blue eyes flashing. "On what grounds?"

"On the inappropriateness of my 'unfortunate marital status.'" Penelope could not keep the bitterness from her voice as she used the exact term that he'd thrown at her.

"Oh." Lady Bursbury purred out the word and a slow, devious smile blossomed over her lips. "Well then, perhaps we shall have to see you wed, my darling Penelope."

And that was exactly what Penelope had been dreading. It was bad enough to tell one's mother that a marriage might be the only thing to allow Penelope back at St. Thomas's. It was worse still when one's mother was a self-proclaimed matchmaker.

2

MacKenzie straightened the small gold "W" pin on his lapel and entered Ashbury Place. The Wicked Earls' Club had welcomed him into their establishment, exactly as Alistair had predicted. And, fortunately, several would be in attendance at the ball.

Including Lord Kendal.

Golden light spilled from grand windows and lent a warmth to the icy night air as music and laughter tinkled through the thick glass.

"Oh, James." Gemma's eyes sparkled like diamonds as she took it all in from her wheeled chair. "It's been a considerable amount of time since I've been to a ball."

"Likewise," MacKenzie muttered, feeling far less excited about the prospect than Gemma did. He'd participated in balls a lifetime ago and held no fond memories.

Long-lashed eyes slid his way upon the caller's announcement of their arrival and he knew he had the attention of the ton. Or at least the fairer sex portion of it. More specifically, the debutantes. And their mothers.

This was why he was here, was it not? To open himself to their onslaught as a means of avoiding—

"Ah, Lady Chatsmore is in attendance." Gemma raised her hand and offered a delicate wave at a willowy woman with a mouth that was as wide as her nose was long.

Something inside MacKenzie withered and died. Just a little. Enough to make him regret the whole bloody idea to attend the Ashbury's ball.

Lady Chatsmore's face immediately brightened as she waved someone to her side. Most likely Judith.

Damn.

She had been a mistake. All of the women MacKenzie had met in England had been a mistake. They sniffed him out by the scent of his wealth and lingered with feigned interest he had been naïve enough to believe was about him.

"If you wanted to escape, now would be the time," Gemma whispered up at him. "Perhaps seek out a few more eligible ladies, hmmm?"

MacKenzie scanned the area for someone he knew. Anyone. Even as he did so, Lady Chatsmore hastened through the room with not only Lady Judith in tow, but also the youngest daughter, Lady Dinah.

"Oakhurst." A strong hand clapped MacKenzie on the shoulder and spun him around.

The man was slightly taller than average with thick black hair combed rakishly back. His blue eyes were narrowed as if in thought and his mouth quirked at the corners in a show of bemusement. In all the years MacKenzie had known him, he'd always maintained a similar expression, guarding his emotions behind a debonair mask.

"Kendal." MacKenzie clasped hands with his old friend.

The earl put an arm around MacKenzie's shoulder and led him away. "Come, there is someone I must introduce you to."

MacKenzie allowed his friend to guide him toward the other

side of the expansive room, where clusters of men stood about with snifters cupped in their gloved hands. "Yer timing is impeccable."

"I know," Kendal drawled. "Still running whisky?"

Such a simple question for such a complicated matter. MacKenzie's whisky smuggling days had ended three years prior when Alistair became the Earl of Benton. But Kendal had run his own underground operation back then. "It's all dried up."

Kendal tilted his head. "Pity."

"How are yer own operations progressing?" MacKenzie asked.

The corners of Kendal's lips twitched a little higher. "Nefarious as ever." He rubbed a gloved finger over the golden "W," buffing it so it gleamed.

"I do actually have someone to introduce you to." Kendal led MacKenzie toward the rear of the room. "A second to sponsor your seat in Parliament."

The caller was still bellowing names of the last, straggling guests in the background. The current one ringing out through the room caused several of the men to lift their eyes to the entryway. MacKenzie followed their gazes and immediately found what had attracted their attention: a woman.

Not just any woman. One with glossy red hair elegantly plaited up and pinned into place with a dozen glittering gems. Her skin was like cream; her body slender and impossibly graceful in her sapphire-blue gown. And though nearly everyone in the room watched her as she walked, she didn't appear to care a whit.

One man in particular regarded the woman with a smirk, as if he found her tardiness amusing. It was to that very man Kendal steered MacKenzie.

"Bursbury," Kendal called.

The gentleman turned to them with an affable grin. "Lord Oakhurst, I presume."

"Indeed," Kendal replied. "Oakhurst, this beast of a man is the

Earl of Bursbury. Don't ever try to take him at any sport. You'll lose, no matter how good you are."

Bursbury laughed at that and didn't bother to deny the claim as he extended a hand toward MacKenzie. He was older, with strands of silver showing in his dark hair and an easy smile. "I've had many a fine whisky in my life, most of which was no doubt provided at risk to your neck. Thank you for that effort." There was a casual ease about him that bespoke of confidence.

"I always appreciate when a man has exemplary taste in whisky." MacKenzie extended his hand in greeting and was pleased when the man took it, despite MacKenzie's thick Scottish accent.

The ton was not always so accepting. At least among the Wicked Earls, many knew of his past transgressions, as well as his previous employment as a valet. It hadn't mattered. Not among them, at least.

"My wife has been friends with Lady Oakhurst for some years," Lord Bursbury said. "I imagine your grandmother is pleased to see you returned."

"Indeed she is," MacKenzie agreed. "Though she's already trying to push me toward marriage."

Bursbury chuckled and shook his head in understanding.

"The curse of us all." Kendal smirked. "I'll never let a woman pin me down."

At this, Bursbury scoffed and nudged the man with his elbow, to which Kendal simply narrowed his eyes further in challenge.

Bursbury regarded MacKenzie. "I have rather an odd question for you. Does Lady Oakhurst's gout still plague her?"

That was indeed an odd question. But the man did mean to sponsor MacKenzie for a seat in parliament. And answering questions of Gemma's gout was preferable to any conversation MacKenzie might have with Lady Judith.

"Aye, she's been in pain with it since my arrival two days prior," MacKenzie replied. "Why do ye ask?"

"I might have a way to ease her discomfort." Bursbury smiled broadly at him.

"You know about gout?" Kendal asked in a bored drawl.

"No, not me." Bursbury gazed out of the sea of faces and beamed as his eyes alighted on his focus of attention. "But she does."

MacKenzie followed his gaze to the woman who had entered the ball so late. Her arms were folded over her chest and she looked quite misplaced. But how could a woman like her not fit in at a ball?

"Who is she?" MacKenzie queried.

"My daughter," Bursbury replied with a proud grin. "Come, I'll make the necessary introductions."

"Are ye trying to play matchmaker?" MacKenzie eyed the man warily.

"Not with that one." Kendal considered the woman from across the room. "She refuses to marry anyone."

Bursbury shrugged with indifference, and despite MacKenzie's better judgement, he found himself being led in the direction of the most beautiful woman in the room.

MacKenzie definitely should have known better.

PENELOPE REMEMBERED WHY SHE HATED BALLS. THE CONSTANT chatter around her, the watered-down lemonade that left an unpleasant tartness lingering at the back of her tongue, the prowling dandies on the lookout for a woman to bail them out of their debts. The list was endless.

Obliviously, her mother spoke excitedly with a woman, both of whom paused periodically to laugh at some jest. Penelope suppressed a sigh to avoid appearing rude. But she *wanted* to sigh. A great, heaving exhale that would billow the ridiculous feathers of the turban of the woman in front of her. More than that, Penelope longed to scream.

It was all so unfair that she had to be here in a ridiculous gown she'd let her mother dress her in to find a husband she did not care for. She wished to be home in the quiet comfort of her library with a stolen glass of brandy in hand as she pored over medical texts.

Her heart crumpled at the reality of the situation. For it had not been a week for Dr. Bailey to make good on this threat. It had taken only two days. Dr. Cooper had sent a formal letter to Penelope excusing her from her volunteer duties at St. Thomas's.

Dr. Cooper had also seen to it that no other hospital would allow her to volunteer either. Which left the home for wounded soldiers as the only source of medical aid she could offer. It was run by Mr. Graston, a Waterloo soldier she had aided in recovering from his time at Bedlam. They had been friends ever since. Most of the veteran soldiers at the home he ran required little assistance, if any at all.

This time, Penelope did sigh. The plumes on the turban of the woman in front of her ruffled in agitation.

"You're far too pretty to be sequestered with us old women." The words were voiced from beside Penelope.

She turned to find an older woman in a wheeled chair. The woman's face was familiar. Perhaps one of her mother's friends?

The lavender gown she wore bespoke of half mourning and her propped foot indicated something Penelope knew quite well. Gout.

"I'm not one for dancing," Penelope confessed.

"Nor am I." The woman indicated her propped leg. "At least, not anymore."

"Might I ask what it is that troubles you?" Penelope asked, though she was certain she already knew.

"Simply an affliction of an old woman." The lady waved her hand, indicating she had no wish to discuss it further.

Drat. It had been over a week since Penelope had been able to attend the hospital. She knew she would miss it, but hadn't anticipated how much it would dig at her very soul.

"Where is your husband?" the woman asked.

Penelope kept from grimacing. "I am unwed."

The woman tilted her head up to Penelope. "How are you not yet married, my dear?"

From a conversation of interest to the most loathsome question in the world. Penelope did her best not to wilt under the inquiry.

"Forgive me," Penelope said politely. "I don't believe we've been introduced."

"Lady Oakhurst," the woman said apologetically. "Do forgive me for my poor manners. I'm old and ill and could not help but approach when I saw you standing alone. You're far too lovely to be off the dance floor, if you don't mind me saying."

Penelope's cheeks flushed with heat at Lady Oakhurst's effusive demeanor.

"I confess, I had a selfish reason for approaching you as well." Lady Oakhurst gave Penelope a coy smile. "My grandson is in town, you see. The Earl of Oakhurst. Perhaps you've met him already?"

Ah, a grandmother set on finding her grandson a wife. No doubt Penelope's mother would find herself in a similar circumstance one day. If Penelope's sister, Eugenia, wed and had children. For Penelope certainly would not.

"I have not yet had the pleasure of meeting Lord Oakhurst," she replied.

"Lord Oakhurst, you say?" Penelope's father came around, grinning at her. "Imagine the luck of it, I have him right here."

"Oh." Penelope stammered. "How...delightful."

A man appeared beside her father, standing at almost the same height. His hair was immaculately combed with the exception of a lock that fell over his forehead. He eyed her not with interest, as did most men, but with an element of wariness.

Interesting.

"Lord Oakhurst, may I present my daughter, Lady Penelope." Lord Bursbury winked at her as if he was not offering her up on a platter to be sent off for marriage. Lord Oakhurst inclined his head. "Well met, Lady Penelope."

His accent was not that of a proper Englishman, but a Scotsman.

She almost blurted out her realization, but had enough years of etiquette at her back to stay her tongue. Instead, she simply lowered her head and politely acknowledged the introduction.

Silence descended uncomfortably over their small group and was made all the more awkward by the expectant stares from Lord Bursbury and Lady Oakhurst. Heavens! Did they expect Penelope and Lord Oakhurst to fall into one another's arms, mad with immediate love?

The very idea twisted in the hollowness of her chest.

"Have you been in London long, my lord?" Penelope asked her question at exactly the same time that Lord Oakhurst extended an invitation to dance.

"I'd love to," Penelope said smoothly, even though she would like anything more than being trapped on the dance floor with an apparent suitor.

He offered her his arm and she accepted—as good, obedient girls do—and allowed him to lead her to the dance floor. They took their places, and the opening notes of the quadrille tumbled through the air.

Lord Oakhurst offered her an uncomfortable quirk of a smile that said he wasn't any more thrilled to be dancing than her. Maybe he was not a suitor after all.

They came together as the steps dictated and his large gloved hands folded over hers. He had a light smoky scent about him. It wasn't the expensive, perfumed aroma most men purchased, but something woodsy and pleasing.

"Yer father introduced ye to me for a reason," he said.

"Oh?" Penelope lifted a brow. "Would it be too bold to assume that reason was marriage?"

They turned to regard the small audience watching them like cats eyeing a twitching mouse tail. At once, Lady Oakhurst, Lord Bursbury and—drat it all, now Lady Bursbury as well—all spun away.

Lord Oakhurst regarded Penelope once more, his face so stricken, so helpless, she nearly laughed. The music pulled them apart for a moment to link arms with other dancers in their square before bringing them together once more.

"I apologize for my father's boldness." She leveled her eyes at his to convey her sincerity. "And in advance for my mother. Feel free to flee at any moment. I won't blame you a bit."

"Actually, yer father introduced us due to yer knowledge of gout," Lord Oakhurst began. "Do ye know much of it?"

The cloud over Penelope lifted somewhat. "I have quite a bit of knowledge and considerable experience from my time at St. Thomas's." To women, her statement would be boastful and proud. But men were different creatures, ones who found confidence to be truth and any faltering to be weak.

The dance had them separate once more and attach themselves to other partners. As she danced with an older gentleman, she realized Lord Oakhurst really was most likely approaching her about his grandmother's gout. And if that were the case, she would have a reason to plunge back into medicine, even as she worked around her present conundrum of being without a husband.

She spun around and into Lord Oakhurst's strong, sure hold once more. Only this time, she eagerly anticipated their continued dance and hoped to expand a bit more on the fascinating topic of gout.

3

M ackenzie wasn't the finest dancer. It was a fact he'd never cared about or even put much thought toward. At least, not until he danced with the likes of Lady Penelope Keats, who seemed to glide effortlessly through the steps with a grace that made him feel as ungainly as an ox.

"What is it ye do at hospital?" he asked, continuing their conversation.

They spun around and he caught the delicate scent of roses, sweet and sensual. It was a fresh smell, like that of the actual flower. Not the sickly-sweet perfume so many ladies insisted on dousing on themselves.

Lady Penelope spun around and came to a stop before him. "I do everything, such as listening to the heart to determine health. I see to people who are having an apoplexy when one arises. I've pulled bullets and glass from wounds." She slipped away to another partner and was returned back to him, her face practically glowing.

"I dinna realize St. Thomas's employed women." He'd meant the statement to be a compliment, but the demure lowering of her gaze, shutting him off from her, told him he'd made a grave mistake.

"I imagine it is verra difficult for a woman," he tried again. "It's always been so for women in the medical field. I'm sure ye've heard of Agnodice."

Recognition did not show on her face. Pity.

"We've not been introduced," Lady Penelope replied.

"She died a long time ago." MacKenzie chuckled. "She lived in ancient Greece and wanted to help women in their delivery of children into the world. In order to practice, she cut her hair to look like a man."

Lady Penelope notched her chin a smidge higher, her eyes bright with interest. "Was she discovered?"

MacKenzie nodded. "But the women of Athens came to her defense and the law barring women from medical practice was lifted."

"For all of our advances in our society, we certainly have crawled backward." There was an understandable edge of bitterness to her voice.

"Ye must be verra good at medical practice to break through the barriers laid before ye." He spun her around.

"I am." She lifted her head with determined confidence. "I have volunteered my time there for the last three years. Not as a physician, or a surgeon, or even a barber. Only as a volunteer. Many there do not relish the presence of a woman among them. I have been recently informed I cannot return until my marital status has become less 'unfortunate.'"

"Unfortunate?" He lifted a brow.

"I'm single when society deems I ought to be wed." She turned to another partner and spun about before returning to him.

He recalled what Kendal had said of her, how she'd declined every offer of marriage thus far. "Ye dinna wish to wed?"

A pained expression put a small line on her otherwise smooth brow. "Precisely. It is a man's ocean and I am but a woman cast upon its waves. But when a woman does not want marriage or children, what is she to do, but try to swim alone?" The small muscles of her neck stood out with her sigh. "It would appear I am losing even that freedom, which is why I must finally concede to seek out a husband."

The music wound down to a close and they took their places across from one another to bow and curtsey. He offered his arm to her to walk her back to her father.

"I believe it's why my father introduced us." Lady Penelope walked at his side with the same elegant grace she had danced with, effortless and beautiful. "Do forgive him. He only seeks to make me happy."

MacKenzie studied her from the corner of his eye, this woman who wished to have a role in a man's ocean, as she put it, who sounded as though she deserved that role more than most men.

"I think he means for ye to aid my grandmother," MacKenzie replied. "Did she discuss her gout with ye?"

"Of course not," she rushed on. "She's far too proper for that. I noticed it myself, but only because I spent most of my time at St. Thomas's specializing in the affliction. Well, that and mesmerizing."

Mesmerizing? What the devil was that?

"I can help her," Lady Penelope offered, her eyes full of hope.

"If it wouldna be any trouble." They were walking slowly now, prolonging the moment when she would be delivered to her father.

"Not at all." She tilted her head becomingly and the gems in her fire-red hair twinkled like stars. "It would be entirely my pleasure to do so."

"Tomorrow then?" MacKenzie suggested. "Ye can come by for tea with her and discuss how ye could offer yer assistance."

"I'll be there." Lady Penelope smiled at him, a genuine smile that made her pale blue eyes glint like a summer sky.

"Thank ye for the dance," he said.

Several men lingered by her father, their stares fixed on Lady Penelope. She must have seen them at the same time as MacKenzie, for her steps slowed almost to a halt. The energy and brilliance drained from her for a breath of a second, but in a blink it returned, replaced by a straight back and perfunctory smile.

"Wish me luck in my search for a husband I do not want," she said between unmoving lips.

"Ye have yer pick of them." He hadn't meant to say it so sarcastically, and yet there it was—stated with weighted cynicism.

"Is it cruel?" she asked abruptly.

"Cruel?"

"To wed someone simply for the benefit of marriage, without knowing or caring for them?" Her lips pressed together in contemplation. "It is cruel," she answered of her own accord.

"It is the way of society, my dear lass." With that, MacKenzie delivered Lady Penelope to her father and bowed to her before making his departure.

Gemma had watched the exchange with a fan fluttering beneath her flushed face. He fetched a glass of lemonade before making his way back to her. She took it with a grateful smile.

"You've always been such a good grandson, James." She paused for a delicate sip. "Tell me everything of your dance with Lady Penelope. She is such a delightful young lady, is she not? I've heard she's extraordinarily accomplished. Not only can she paint with the skill of an artist, but she sings like an angel."

"She also has medical knowledge," MacKenzie replied. "Specifically, on gout."

"Does she?" Gemma lifted her brows. "Accomplished, beautiful and skilled." Exhaustion lined her eyes and the stiff-backed, regal way she'd sat in her chair upon arrival had begun to wilt.

"I've asked her to come to tea tomorrow to speak with ye." MacKenzie reached to take Gemma's empty lemonade glass from her. "Shall we take our leave?"

She pressed the small glass in her hands for a moment, and met his eyes. "You could do worse than her, James."

At that exact moment, Lady Penelope sailed by them on the dance floor, graceful and lovely. Alabaster skin, pink lips, auburn hair, pale blue eyes and a confidence that would rattle most men.

But James MacKenzie wasn't most men.

"James." A familiar, feminine voice rankled over his skin like a chill.

He turned slowly in the direction of Lady Judith and waited for all the years of angst and hurt to slam into him. Except they did not.

She smiled up at him, her smooth lips pulling back to reveal her small, white teeth as she batted her lovely brown eyes at him. "It's been years."

He gazed at her for a moment and still not a modicum of emotion whispered through him. Apparently seven years and countless instances of eight glasses of whisky were enough to remove her from his heart. Thank God.

"Condolences on the loss of yer betrothed." He bowed formally. "Lady Judith."

"Thank you." She let her gaze rove over him. "You may call me Judith," she said sweetly. "I believe our past association would allow a lack of formality. And perhaps our future as well..."

Emotion did edge in on him then, a white-hot flicker of anger. The closeness they shared had been a kiss, the confession of wondering at a life together, and then immediately following the death of MacKenzie's uncle: her betrothal to Gilbert.

"I fear that wouldna be proper, Lady Judith." He bowed again. "Do excuse me."

"Father says you are considering a betrothal to me." She caught the crook of his arm in what was obviously intended to be an endearing grasp. He saw it for what it was: entrapment.

MacKenzie squared his shoulders. "Ye've heard wrong, Lady

Judith." He pulled his arm delicately from her grasp. "If ye'll excuse me..."

He inclined his head and stepped to take his leave.

"Why?" The agreeable expression melted from her face and pulled the corners of her lips downward. "Why would you not do what is right? I am meant to be the Countess of Oakhurst."

"Are ye aware I was another earl's valet for the last three years?" He squared his shoulders, expecting her scorn. "For a friend, after he inherited his earldom some years after we'd met."

"I'd heard." Her gaze slipped away momentarily. He'd unsettled her. Good.

Still, she pushed out her chest. "I can forego some gossip, as I'm sure you can imagine." She leaned closer and spoke with an edge to her voice. "The title belongs to me. I've waited seven years, James. Seven years. I've earned it, regardless what you've done in your past."

But it was not his past that troubled him so much as hers. And what she'd done to him.

As he watched, Lady Penelope was led to the dance floor in the distance on the arm of yet another gentleman. MacKenzie shifted his attention back to Lady Judith and answered earnestly, "Forgive me. I am already considering another lady."

❦

THE BULK OF PENELOPE'S BLACK MEDICAL BAG WAS A WELCOME weight against her thigh. She kept it close to her side as she and her mother rode to Oakhurst Place, and had politely declined the footman's offer to secure it outside the carriage.

As they traveled the short distance, Penelope considered what she might be up against with regard to Lady Oakhurst's foot. Advanced stages were far more difficult to treat. Urate crystals were insidious things that would eventually mutilate a foot. At that stage and beyond, the bones could never be the same. Hopefully, the dowager countess was not so far along in her affliction.

"The Earl of Oakhurst is quite a handsome man," Lady Bursbury said suddenly.

Penelope shifted her concentration from her experiences with gout to recall the man she'd met the prior evening. "Is he?"

In truth, she hadn't noticed. He was tall with dark hair and eyes and appeared to be rather fit. Not all the men she'd danced with had possessed such appealing qualities. In that regard, she could see how one would find him attractive.

"Oh, Penelope," Lady Bursbury exclaimed. "Do try. If nothing else, he was the only one you seemed to speak to with any amount of interest."

"His conversation was the most interesting." Penelope almost smiled at his mention of the Greek woman who had broken through the barriers of men. "He had a pleasant scent about him."

Lady Bursbury nodded.

Penelope tried hard, recalling the sharp line of his jaw and high cheekbones. "He was rather handsome," Penelope conceded.

At this, her mother brightened. "Oh, I knew you thought so too."

Penelope had not actually, at least until this moment of reflection, but refrained from stating as much.

"And he invited you to attend to Lady Oakhurst this afternoon." Her mother's eyes widened with obvious excitement. "I believe he's quite taken with you," she said in a singsong voice she reserved for moments of pure anticipation.

Thankfully at that moment, the carriage pulled to a stop before Oakhurst Place. Within minutes, they were led up the stairs to the drawing room.

Tea had already been laid out on the polished wood table, with delicate cups resting on small saucers with dainty blue flowers painted upon their glossy surfaces. Except there were not three cups.

There were four.

It appeared Lord Oakhurst would be joining them, a suspicion that was echoed in her mother's nudge against Penelope's side.

Before she could shoot her mother a disparaging look, the double doors opened and Lord Oakhurst entered, pushing Lady Oakhurst in her wheeled chair. Most would expect a servant to attend to the older woman, but the earl seemed content with the task.

Nor was that all he did for her. Penelope had seen him bring his grandmother a glass of lemonade at the ball. It was a rare kindness for him to care for her as he did.

The four of them exchanged pleasantries and settled down to tea with Lady Oakhurst across from Lady Bursbury and Lord Oakhurst opposite Penelope.

It was a different thing to see a person in the light of day when one had only known them in a candlelit ballroom. If Penelope had presumed Lord Oakhurst to be attractive the evening before, she knew him now to be as her mother declared: handsome.

His hands were large; his fingers blunted where he pinched the narrow handle of the teacup in a tenuous grasp.

His eyes were not dark as Penelope had assumed, but a deep moss green. The bit of hair that had fallen over his brow the evening before, she now could see was a stubborn lock that curled forward when the rest was combed smoothly into place. It was boyishly endearing when the rest of him was so decidedly masculine in every way.

But Lord Oakhurst was not the subject of her visit at Oakhurst Place. She needed to refocus her attention on his grandmother and how she might address the topic of seeing to the afflicted toe.

Having never done medical house calls before, Penelope was unsure how best to go about bringing up the topic. She was just trying to piece together a way she could introduce it into the current conversation about the weather when Lord Oakhurst announced it for her.

"Once we've finished our tea, I imagine Lady Penelope would like to see to yer foot, Grandmother." He turned his green eyes toward Penelope. "If that's amenable to ye."

Penelope nodded with relief. "Of course. I have everything I need here. Would you prefer I attend to you in your private chamber?" Heat effused Penelope's cheeks as she regarded Lady Oakhurst. "I confess, I have only ever seen to patients at St. Thomas's."

"That would be most agreeable," Lady Oakhurst said.

After it was settled that Penelope would see to Lady Oakhurst while Lady Bursbury remained downstairs, Lord Oakhurst took it upon himself to carry his grandmother to her chamber.

Once he'd delivered her carefully into a chair close to where Penelope had set her black bag, he lingered. "I'd like to stay, if that's fine with ye, Gemma." He pursed his lips together. "Grandmother," he amended.

Penelope bit back a grin at the endearment. She had known the former Earl of Oakhurst, the profligate who had been found dead and partially naked in the Serpentine with a woman of ill repute. She hadn't been acquainted with the Dowager Lady Oakhurst then, but no grandmother wanted to be made aware of such things in regard to their own grandson. Penelope was pleased to see the new Lord Oakhurst made up where his predecessor had so painfully failed.

"It's well and good with me." Lady Oakhurst warmed under her grandson's concern. "Though you should know it's terribly unsightly."

"I assure ye, I've seen worse." Lord Oakhurst winked at her and settled into a chair some feet away.

It was an odd thing to be in someone's private quarters, being that it was so intimately personal. Penelope put aside her genteel modesty and focused instead as a physician. She gently lifted the lavender silk of Lady Oakhurst's gown to reveal a naked foot.

The older woman flushed with embarrassment. "It pains me terribly."

"Wearing a slipper would most likely make you lose consciousness." Penelope studied the pink, shiny skin along the side of Lady Oakhurst's foot, relieved to find it was absent the bony knob of a long-term sufferer. "You needn't apologize. How many days has this bout been affecting you?"

"Five," Lord Oakhurst replied for his grandmother. It was then Penelope noticed him leaning forward to watch what she did. "Is there a wrap? A poultice? Anything that might help?"

"She is nearly at the end of the worst of it," Penelope explained. "Generally an attack will last seven days at most." She went on to detail remedies that proved most efficacious: drinking tart cherry juice once a day, avoiding rich foods and spirits when possible, introducing light exercise once the pain dissipated. In the meantime, she provided them with a tonic of meadowsweet root and a drop of poppy juice to take the edge off the pain and delivered a dose to demonstrate how much to give.

It was not Lady Oakhurst who listened intently to all of the discourse of instructions, though she did bemoan the bit about rich food and spirits. It was Lord Oakhurst who followed all of the details and nodded his ascent to ensure it would happen.

He accepted the tincture with thanks. "I appreciate ye taking time from yer day to share yer knowledge with us."

His compliment was considerate and greatly appreciated. It was not often she received praise for her hard-won learning. Not when so many people were opposed to seeing a woman in a man's role.

"It is kind of you to look after her," Penelope said. "Most would abandon the task to their servants."

He glanced regretfully at Lady Oakhurst whose eyes had gone somewhat glassy with the effects of the poppy juice. "I have abandoned her long enough already." He indicated the door and followed Penelope to it. "I'll no' make that same mistake again."

She allowed him to lead her from Lady Oakhurst's Chamber.

"I should like to speak with ye on another matter, if ye can spare a moment," he said.

"Of course." Lady Penelope faced him in the quiet hallway.

He was taller than her by at least a good foot, which put her brow somewhere around the middle of his broad chest. She noticed his height when they'd danced together, but hadn't appreciated it the way she did now when they were alone.

"I dinna mean to cause offense," he said in a low voice. The delicate burr of his brogue hummed in the air and tickled through her veins. "But what I mean to ask ye is quite improper."

4

MacKenzie had carefully considered what exactly he would say to Lady Penelope once he had her alone. It had all gone perfectly in his mind. Until the very moment when he needed to open his mouth and say it aloud.

"Improper?" She tilted her head with evident curiosity.

"Aye." He shifted his weight. "Ye see, I've no' gone to yer da first. I dinna want him to make a decision for ye."

Any tension in her expression smoothed. "Whatever you mean to ask me, you're off to a good start."

He shifted his weight back to the other foot and his thoughts all jumbled together. Good God. Why was he so bloody nervous? It was only a damn marriage proposal.

The only one he'd ever done.

To a woman who had rejected every other man who had asked her.

Bloody hell.

Her brows pinched together. "What is it you mean to ask me?"

"Will ye marry me?" The question came out in a clumsy tumble that made him wince inwardly.

She blinked in surprise. And no wonder. No doubt the ungain-liness of it hit her like an unexpected blow.

"I beg your pardon?" she said slowly.

"That dinna come out right." He smiled apologetically, which she returned with a look of brilliant relief.

He steeled himself for the second round. He'd lied to Runners on whisky runs, smooth-talked his way around rough situations, and gone this long without letting a woman rattle his nerves like a bad toss of dice.

God, she smelled good. Garden-grown roses, the kind that smelled sweetest in the morning with a frosting of dew on their open petals.

A frosting of dew? What the devil was the matter with him?

"Ye need to wed," he said carefully. "So ye can return to the hospital, aye?"

The skin around her eyes tensed, but she did not stop him.

Be calm, MacKenzie. He weighed each word before he finally spoke again. "If I dinna find a new wife, there will be expectations that I resume my cousin's betrothal to Lady Judith."

Her mouth quirked. Ah, so she at least understood his predicament.

"Ye'd mentioned ye thought it cruel to convince a man to wed ye simply so ye could return to the hospital."

She nodded, as she no doubt recalled their conversation.

"I dinna want a wife, but I need one," he said finally.

"I see." Her pale blue eyes were sharp with intelligence and had not once left his face as she listened to his terribly awkward proposal.

"Ye would have yer freedom to return to the hospital, and comfort in that ye are knowingly with a man ye dinna have to love," he said.

"And you would be released of the obligation to wed your cousin's fiancée by marrying a woman you do not have to love," she concluded.

A woman he did not have to love. Aye, that was exactly what he wanted. For where there was love, there was pain.

Like Lady Judith had hurt him so long ago by choosing Gilbert's title over MacKenzie. Like all the fickle women who fawned over MacKenzie once he was heir presumptive. He didn't want a woman who was only interested in him for title or money, and he certainly didn't want a woman who would put his heart at risk to get it. Not again.

The tension bled away from MacKenzie's shoulders. "Aye. That's it exactly."

She pressed her lips together. "Would I be required to attend balls and social gatherings?"

"God, I hope neither of us have to," he muttered. "However, I suppose some will be required from time to time. Only those of great import."

She leaned her head to the side as though conceding to the logic of his begrudging point.

A maid came down the hall and MacKenzie pressed his hand to Lady Penelope's lower back to guide her toward the stairs so as not to arouse suspicion.

"Would children be required?" Lady Penelope asked quietly as they descended the stairs one slow step at a time.

"Nay." MacKenzie offered a silent apology to Gemma, who no doubt would love children in the house again. A marriage such as the one he was contriving with Lady Penelope would do best without offspring.

"Good." Lady Penelope offered a flash of a smile. "And what of me? Will you dictate my comings and goings?"

MacKenzie shook his head. "But if ye take a lover, I'd prefer ye exercise discretion."

He would in no way force Lady Penelope to be intimate with him, not physically or through marital coercion.

She chuckled at that. "There will be no lovers. I have no interest in such things."

"Everyone has interest in such things."

She stopped at the landing and turned that bright, intelligent gaze on him fully once more. "I do not."

"Verra well."

"And you will, as well?" She flicked her stare away briefly, the only indication thus far of any discomfort with their discussion. "Be discreet with your lovers, I mean?"

The idea of taking a woman to bed while married to another did not sit well with him. And yet the thought of never again having a woman in his bed held even less appeal.

What the devil was he getting himself into?

He nodded.

"There we have it," she agreed. "I shall be happy to marry you."

"Would you prefer that I get a special license?" he asked. "Doing so would allow the affair to be more private." Not only would the license allow them the ability to have the wedding performed away from prying eyes, but they could have the ceremony whenever they bloody well wanted. No waiting on banns to be called, or any other such nonsense.

"That would be ideal, thank you." Lady Penelope held out her hand to him. She wore no gloves this time and he noted the slenderness of her long fingers that tapered at the ends. "Then it appears we have an agreement, Lord Oakhurst."

He took her hand in his and found it cool against the heat of his own palm. He leaned over and kissed the tops of her small knuckles. "I'll see to it once I've spoken with yer father." The fresh rose perfume of her teased at his awareness once more.

He straightened, not wanting to find appeal in the way she smelled. "I will call on him later today."

"Very well." Lady Penelope nodded at the conclusion of their contracted union. "Good day to you, Lord Oakhurst."

"Good day, Lady Penelope."

It was most likely not the typical farewell for a couple recently engaged. But for them, it was adequate.

She strode off, carried away by footsteps that made it appear as if she floated over the smooth marble flooring. He considered her as she departed. Gemma was right: Penelope was indeed extraordinary. She was logical and pragmatic. The ideal choice for a wife to guarantee he would never again fall in love.

Upon taking their leave from Oakhurst Place, Penelope climbed into the carriage, nearly ready to burst with her news. She had tried to reconcile herself to the idea of marriage ever since she'd come out, but it had never settled properly on her. Though Lady Bursbury had ceased mentioning the notion of a husband some time ago, it was obvious she still hoped for a marriage for her eldest daughter.

Finally, Penelope would be able to comply with her mother's wishes, to complete the one act in which she'd so dreadfully failed.

"I presume it went well based on your elated expression." Lady Bursbury reached a gloved hand across the small carriage and squeezed Penelope's wrist. "You're brilliant, darling. I'm so very proud of you. If I don't tell you often enough, I want to make sure you know it without a modicum of doubt."

Oh, and Penelope did know it. Her mother told her all the time. Almost every afternoon that she met Penelope at St. Thomas's. And Penelope appreciated it every time. Every. Time. She braced herself as the coach pulled forward to return them to Bursbury Place at the end of the lane of townhouses.

"You'll be even prouder of me now." Penelope gave a little bounce in her seat. Yes, a little bounce in her seat, though she could scarcely recall ever having done anything of the sort in her entire life. Truly the excitement of fulfilling her mother's greatest wish was practically beyond comprehension.

Lady Bursbury pressed her hands together over her breast. "Did you discover a way to cure Lady Oakhurst?"

"It isn't that," Penelope said dismissively. "Although, yes, Lady Oakhurst will heal in time if she follows my instructions."

Confusion crinkled her mother's brow. "Whatever could have you in such a state, then?"

"I'm getting married," Penelope blurted out.

She had expected her mother to crow with happiness, for the crowning victory finally achieved. She had expected a great hug as wedding plans immediately spilled forth from years of sequestered, secret plans. She had expected, well, anything more than she received.

Lady Bursbury blinked. "I beg your pardon?"

"I'm getting married, Mama," Penelope repeated. "To Lord Oakhurst."

Her mother's mouth worked silently for a moment before words finally emerged. "I wasn't aware you were so well acquainted," she stammered. "You...love him then?"

Penelope shook her head. "No, which is why it's so capital. He doesn't want a wife any more than I want a husband and yet we both must wed. It's an ideal situation to prevent us from having to hurt people who *do* wish a proper union."

The light faded from Lady Bursbury's eyes and her shoulders drooped forward. In fact, all of her seemed to wither. Lines showed on her face that Penelope had never noticed, arching around the sides of her mouth and crinkling alongside her eyes.

"Oh, Penelope," she said softly. It was unlike any way she'd spoken her eldest daughter's name before. Not with chastisement or teasing admonishment, but with genuine...disappointment.

Penelope's heart crumpled at the desolate sound. "I thought you'd be pleased," she whispered.

Lady Bursbury shook her head slowly and tears swam in her eyes. Actual tears.

"Mama." Penelope reached for her mother.

"You deserve to be *loved*." The carriage drew to a stop before their townhouse and Lady Bursbury touched her gloved hands to her eyes, blotting away her tears.

The door opened and a blast of frigid air swept in. Penelope and her mother emerged from the carriage and rushed from the chill into Bursbury Place.

"Elias," Lady Bursbury cried as soon as they were in the townhouse. "Elias."

Lord Bursbury came clattering down the stairs with Penelope's sister, Eugenia, at his heels.

Lady Bursbury ran to him, still clad in her coat and hat. "Penelope is going to marry Lord Oakhurst."

He pumped his fist in the air. "I knew it. On my honor, I saw that man and knew he'd be a match fit for our Penny."

"No." Lady Bursbury backed away from him, stricken. "How could you? She doesn't even *love* him."

With that, she raced up the stairs mid-sob.

Silence followed her dramatic departure.

Lord Bursbury grimaced. "Well, that didn't go as I'd planned."

Eugenia pressed her hand to her mouth in a poor attempt to suppress a giggle. They were all well aware of Lady Bursbury's theatrics. Everything she did was performed with grandeur. She loved unlike any mother ever did, she gave like no one else could and cared more than it seemed possible for a soul to do. And it was all well and good until her heart broke.

And Penelope had just broken her mother's very large, very fragile heart.

Eugenia pursed her lips. "Does this mean I can have my come out soon?"

Lord Bursbury gently pushed at her shoulder, nudging her back up the stairs. "We'll discuss it later. Go on now."

Eugenia twirled in her white day dress, sending the muslin belling out around her slender frame. She hummed a little song to herself and bounded up the risers, setting her auburn curls bouncing.

Lord Bursbury beckoned Penelope to him. He took her medical bag from her, helped her from her coat and embraced her with all the love and protective comfort only a father could offer. "Is this union what you want, Penny?"

She nodded against his large, solid chest and hated that tears prickled hot in her eyes.

"Then your mother will come around." Lord Bursbury pressed a kiss to the top of Penelope's head and smiled down at her. "Trust me."

As always, Lord Bursbury knew his wife better than anyone else. Within an hour, a gentle rap came at Penelope's bedchamber door and her mother entered, appearing red-eyed and regretful.

"Might I have a word with you?" Lady Bursbury asked.

Penelope moved aside on her large bed, sliding several medical texts with her as she did so to make room for her mother.

"Forgive me, Daughter." Lady Bursbury clenched at a wadded handkerchief and rolled her eyes. "You know how I can be."

Penelope couldn't help but smile at her mother's self-deprecation.

"You are so wonderful, Penelope." Lady Bursbury's eyes watered. "You're intelligent and beautiful and graceful and accomplished. There's nothing you cannot do." She pressed the crumpled hanky to first one eye, then the other. "You deserve someone who can appreciate all those many extraordinary things about you." She sniffled. "You deserve to be loved."

Penelope stared down at the text in front of her, the truth lingering on her tongue until finally, *finally*, after all these years, she admitted aloud her greatest fear. "I don't think I can love in return, Mother."

"Of course you can," Lady Bursbury said. "You love me and

your father, and even Eugenia. In your twenty years, I've never doubted that."

"Oh, I do," she conceded. "Yes, even Eugenia. For the most part." She offered her mother a teasing smile to diffuse the seriousness of the matter. "But romantic love..." She shook her head. "It eludes me. The men are all so dull, so consumed with their own selfish lives: what they've accomplished and what *they* want. None of them desire anything more from a wife than a dowry; for her to be a beautiful accessory for their arm and a few children. How can I love *that*?"

Lady Bursbury's eyes narrowed somewhat in calculating consideration. It was a look Penelope knew well. And it was dangerous.

An anxious knot twisted in the pit of her stomach. "What are you planning to do?"

All the angst eased from her mother's features, bringing back her usual agreeable expression. "I'm going to make Lord Oakhurst fall in love with you." Lady Bursbury puffed out her chest like a robin who'd just plucked the fattest worm. "And in turn, you won't be able to help but fall in love with him."

Penelope opened her mouth to protest, but the look of joy on her mother's face quieted her objection.

After all, Penelope would be able to return to St. Thomas's once she was wed. She and Lord Oakhurst had already declared their indifferent intentions toward one another. What harm could possibly come of her mother attempting to make them fall in love?

⁍ 5 ⁋

The management of the earldom was much more daunting than MacKenzie had anticipated. There were the accounts of the house, of course, as well as those at Oakhurst Manor. But there were also the tenants on his land to see to, as well as the complaints forwarded to him by his steward, Mr. Barclay.

He flipped through the pages included with Mr. Barclay's formal account of the estate's dealings. There was a puzzling bit in the agriculture report, citing the progress of the Norfolk four-course system. What the deuce was the Norfolk four-course system?

"You may want to make yourself presentable, James," Gemma said from the doorway. "Your betrothed will arrive soon to take tea with me."

MacKenzie looked up at his grandmother, who was now out of her wheeled chair and back on her cane. Gemma had been elated with the news of MacKenzie's betrothal to Lady Penelope and used every opportunity to refer to her as "his betrothed" with that keen glint in her eye. For her part, Lady Penelope had been by each of the last several days, seeing to Gemma and ensuring she was recovering well from her gout flare.

He nodded to the cane. "Did she give ye permission to be using that?"

"Of course she did." Gemma strode into the room with her cane thumping over the thick Brussels weave carpet. "James, you do look a mess. I don't believe you've even shaved."

She stated the last bit as though it was as appalling as him not donning a shirt.

MacKenzie rubbed a hand over his whiskered jaw. Though he hated to admit it, Alistair had been right in his assumption that MacKenzie would detest the use of a valet. Gemma had forced him into hiring one, an older gentleman who did the job adequately, but it had been difficult to not follow behind him and fold the cravats just so or suggest a different direction of stroke while shaving.

"I forewent the razor this morning as I knew I'd be locked in torment perusing Mr. Barclay's reports," he explained.

"It isn't all that bad." She sank into the seat opposite him. "The reports are always wonderfully detailed. Mr. Barclay is truly a wonder."

MacKenzie grunted. Wonder wasn't the word he would use. Verbose would work. Loquacious, garrulous, effusive. Any of those would be more applicable.

"It doesna make much sense," James confessed. "Details on incomes and expenses, aye, I understand those parts of it. But this agriculture report doesna make a whit of sense. A Norfolk four-course system sounds like a grand method of feeding livestock."

"It is, in a way." Gemma reached for the report. "It's actually a method of resting soil while still keeping it in use. The crops are rotated on an annual basis with the fields all placed in various stages of rotation to ensure they are profitable, and that the livestock have enough available food. We implemented the process six years ago and it has proven to have been a prudent choice."

MacKenzie stared at his grandmother as she went through the

information with the precise detail of a steward. "How the devil do ye know all this, Gemma?"

She scoffed, lifting her chin. "Do you really think Gilbert had any mind for such things? I learned what I needed to protect the Oakhurst legacy. For you, for your children and their children to follow." A soft smile touched her lips as if she could picture those bespoken children at that very moment.

Guilt pinched at MacKenzie. There would be no children in his union with Lady Penelope, but of course he could not tell his grandmother as much.

"I think ye're the wonder, Gemma, not Mr. Barclay." MacKenzie reached across the table and reclaimed the report she had laid aside.

"Women do what they can in this man's world." She pushed herself to her feet.

MacKenzie considered her. "Lady Penelope said something of a similar nature," he muttered absently.

Gemma's eyes sparkled. "I knew I liked her from the first. Lady Bursbury and I have been discussing details for the wedding. I may suggest a Christmastime theme with holly in place of hot house flowers. What do you think?"

MacKenzie looked at Gemma over the top of the report with a grimace. "I think I'd rather learn more about the Norfolk four-course system than discuss flowers."

She laughed good-naturedly and a smile pulled at his lips. Gemma had changed in the short week since Lady Penelope had been seeing to her. Where once she had seemed too fragile, now she was stronger, happier, her sturdiness restored and the absence of pain transforming her back into the Gemma he remembered from his youth.

George appeared in the doorway. "Excuse the interruption." He bowed. "Lady Penelope is here to see you."

Gemma thanked the butler and beckoned MacKenzie. "Come, James. Bid good day to your lovely betrothed."

"I don't look presentable," he protested.

She scrutinized him with a cursory look and pursed her lips. "You don't, but you're coming anyway." There was the tone that he recalled from his childhood, the one that brooked no argument.

He sighed and got to his feet, regretting having foregone his shave that morning, especially since he'd been at Parliament so often, he had not seen Lady Penelope since they had discussed their betrothal. Unfortunately, not seeing her did not mean she hadn't entered his thoughts. She occupied far more of them than he cared to admit.

His mind often wondered about the taste of her lips, the feel of her skin; all the things he would have liberties to as a husband. And all the things they'd agreed not to share. Or had they? He'd been so bloody nervous that he now couldn't recall having decided on the consummation of their marriage.

He led Gemma to the drawing room, steeling himself for the impact of Lady Penelope's beauty. Not that preparation did him any good.

She rose from the plush seat as they entered. Early afternoon light streamed through the window and caught at her hair, turning it fiery red with glints of copper. The smile she gave Gemma turned reticent when it fell on him, as though she didn't know what to do or say around him anymore than he did around her.

Erring on the side of polite conversation was a sensible start. "Good day, Lady Penelope. I trust ye're well?"

"Yes, thank you." Her gaze lingered on his grizzled chin and he cursed himself once more for having forgone his shave.

But then that perceptive stare of hers drifted downward to his lips where it paused before a blush stole over her cheeks and she swiftly met his eyes once more. "And yourself?" she asked.

"Fine," he replied with a nod. "Fine, thank ye."

He tried to set the observation from his mind, and yet he

continued to go back to it. Was she curious about kissing him as well, then?

The idea held considerable appeal.

The room was scented lightly with the fresh perfume of roses and he found himself wondering what part of her smelled so heavenly. Was it her silky hair? The delicate insides of her wrists? The sweet curve between her neck and shoulder? He wanted to nuzzle his mouth over every inch of her creamy skin, discern its exact location so he could breathe her in.

"This afternoon, we'll be settling on a date for the wedding." She fiddled with the handle of her black medical bag and ran a single delicate fingertip over the smooth leather. "I'm grateful my mother and your grandmother are so adept at planning such events. I confess I haven't a mind for any of it."

"Nor have I," MacKenzie admitted.

They chuckled together and a companionable silence descended on the room. "I'll leave ye to it then." He bowed. "Good day, Lady Penelope."

She lowered her head. "Good day, Lord Oakhurst."

He turned then and took his leave. But even as he did, he found he could not as easily extract his thoughts from the exchange. Or from her.

And thinking of one's betrothed when entering a marriage of convenience, he knew, was a very, very bad thing indeed.

◔◔

PENELOPE HAD NOT BEEN POSTURING WHEN SHE TOLD LORD Oakhurst that she had no mind for wedding planning. She attended the informal meetings her mother held to discuss the preparations but offered only enough input to keep a steady smile on her mother's face.

In truth, Penelope suspected Lady Oakhurst and Lady Bursbury enjoyed the freedom to twist the event into whatever creation they deemed appropriate. All Penelope had insisted upon was that it be a private affair, away from the ever-vigilant gaze of the ton.

It was decided the wedding would take place in December, so that a winter theme could be incorporated, adorned with touches of Christmas. Penelope had said that was fine.

They wanted her in a white gown that sparkled like glittering snow. She said that was fine too and read through current medical journals while the modiste fitted her for a gown she scarcely saw.

They wanted holly and other such holiday-appropriate foliage for decor and Penelope said that was also fine. For while they did the planning, she sharpened her skills on the most recent medical practices to ensure she would be of optimal assistance upon her return to St. Thomas's.

Yes. Yes. Yes. It was *all* fine.

Until the limited sands of a week's time trickled through at an ephemeral pace and ran out completely. Penelope had been enjoying an early breakfast, the hour of professional workers as she was wont to do, when Lady Bursbury had entered and cheerfully chirped that the day of the wedding had finally arrived.

Penelope lowered the paper she'd been reading and regarded her mother in shock. "Already?"

Lady Bursbury laughed. "Already? Darling, this week has dragged on at an interminable pace until this very moment."

Penelope regarded the uneaten toast points on her plate. A greasy smear of butter glistened atop the bread, no longer as appealing as it had been only moments ago. "Is Lord Oakhurst aware?"

"Aware of his own wedding?" Lady Bursbury chuckled and shook her head. The red curls on either side of her face fluttered about as she did so. "I would imagine he would be. Come, Penelope. I want to ensure we have an ample amount of time for you to be just perfect before we make our way to the church."

"But it is only half past eight," Penelope exclaimed.

Lady Bursbury was undeterred. "This is the first step in having him fall in love with you."

The way she said it implied there might be several steps. Perhaps many. Enough for Penelope to already dread having not discouraged her mother.

"Come along now." Lady Bursbury sailed out of the room with the obvious expectation that Penelope would follow.

And, of course, she did. As good girls do.

For a small, private wedding, there was certainly a lot that had gone into it. Starting with the gown, which even Penelope had to admit was exquisite. Silver tissue sparkled over the gown, giving it the impression of glittering snow on a sunlit morning. It was simple yet beautiful, thankfully without Brussels lace dripping from every available inch of fabric.

The waist was fashionably nipped in at the center, and white rabbit fur lined a hooded short cloak to give the gown a "more wintery feel" per Lady Bursbury. The modiste had fitted it perfectly to Penelope's trim body, with the cinched waist and ruched bosom making for an admittedly flattering cut.

As it turned out, Lady Bursbury was also correct in starting Penelope's preparations so early. Even Penelope's coming out had not required so much attention to detail. After the gown was put on, her hair was curled and styled with gems twinkling throughout, followed by a touch of rouge applied to her cheeks and lips.

At long last, Lady Bursbury declared her nothing short of sheer perfection. All that remained was a short half hour to get to the chapel where Penelope would wed the Earl of Oakhurst.

They arrived with time to spare, of course. Lady Bursbury had planned every part of the day down to the smallest detail. And it showed.

The tiny chapel had been adorned with gold ribbons and clusters of holly. The pointed dark leaves and sprigs of brilliantly red berries were the ideal complement to the glossy ribbons and gleaming, polished wood of the chapel.

Penelope's favorite decorations, however, were the cut outs of various organs mingling with the gold paper stars. Nancy had clearly remembered the time Penelope had done that several years back at Christmas and had incorporated the memory into the decor of the church. It was a personal touch that only her mother could provide and it touched Penelope's heart.

The congregation was thin of company, but Penelope would have it no other way, wanting only her closest family. Aside from her parents and the dowager Lady Oakhurst, Uncle Noah and his lovely wife, Helen, were in attendance. Eugenia stood as Penelope's bridesmaid, wearing a simple white dress with twists of golden wire shining through her curling auburn hair. She beamed at Penelope and gleamed with girlish excitement at her role in the event.

Penelope, however, was not as eager for her own role. Nervousness spun a nauseating dance in her empty stomach, and she regretted not having eaten the toast points at breakfast. Eugenia might be looking forward to marriage with her fanciful notions of romance, but Penelope was decidedly not.

Panic charged through her veins, as cold as the wind howling outside and just as fierce.

It was a mutually beneficial marriage, one with little expectation. But what if that changed? What if Lord Oakhurst decided he wished to have children? Or became determined that she quit her work at the hospital? Or what if—

The door to the chapel banged open.

Penelope sucked in a breath. No. She wasn't ready. Not yet. Not now.

A warm hand curled around hers. She looked down and found her fingers entwined with her mother's. Lady Bursbury smiled and nodded encouragingly. Just like she had done when Penelope attended her first private tutoring lesson for medicine and was worried that she wouldn't be up to snuff. And then again when she had her come out and feared everyone would find her lacking.

And then later still when she went to St. Thomas's for the first time, when she'd assisted Mr. Graston through the nightmares in his mind those three years ago.

As with all those previous occurrences, the confidence and the love in that simple nod told Penelope all would be well. She straightened her back, lifted her chin and turned to face the man she would marry.

※ 6 ※

MacKenzie knew Lady Penelope to be a beautiful woman, but he hadn't noticed exactly how exquisitely stunning she was until the day of their wedding. Her gown showed off a sensual figure with delicate curves he hadn't noticed before due to the current fashion of high-waisted gowns. The one she wore now was none of those things. No, it was fitted to her slim body, revealing the flare of her hips and a waist so cinched, he found himself tempted to span his hands around it. And though his heart was suddenly racing at an extraordinary rate, she appeared completely serene.

She approached the altar where he stood waiting for her, with Kendal at his place beside MacKenzie as his best man. God, but she was lovely.

"Ye look beautiful," he said softly.

Someone behind them in the nearly empty pews sighed. He scarcely noticed, for at exactly that moment, Lady Penelope's cheeks flushed in a gentle blush. In the short time he'd known her, he hadn't expected Lady Penelope would ever be a woman to blush. But there it was, staining her smooth, porcelain skin the bonniest shade of pink.

It made him wonder if he could make all of her blush so, with his hands, his mouth...

"Thank you." Her light blue gaze flicked over him briefly, paused on his lips, then slid shyly away. "You look quite handsome yourself."

The vicar took that at his cue and began the ceremony. MacKenzie hardly listened to any of it. Once one had attended a wedding, one knew exactly what would be said at the next one. Instead, his mind embraced the very real idea that he would have a wife, someone more than Gemma dependent on him. He would have to redouble his efforts to learn the Norfolk four-stop system or whatever the bloody hell it was called. As well as making the most out of his new parliamentary seat.

Concern for their future well-being was not the only path MacKenzie's mind trod. His attention continually wandered toward Lady Penelope, marveling at her beauty the way one does a painted masterpiece. Her words slipped into his mind from the prior conversation when they had agreed to wed.

There will be no lovers. I have no interest in such things.

He would not touch a woman who did not welcome his affections. Meaning, he might spend a lifetime thus: always looking, never touching. Forever wanting.

She shifted her stare toward him and spoke the words that would forever tie her to him.

Kendal pushed a small gold band into MacKenzie's palm, which MacKenzie promptly slid onto Lady Penelope's slender finger, and repeated his series of words from the vicar. And so, it was done. MacKenzie had married the most beautiful woman in all of London, a woman he knew he would be spared from loving.

The vicar brought out the registry and handed the quill first to MacKenzie to sign, then to Lady Penelope.

No, not Lady Penelope...Lady Oakhurst. *His wife.*

She accepted the pen and signed with a slight tremble that belied her calm exterior. Once the necessary papers had been signed, she straightened and smiled brightly at him. "And we're married."

"So we are," he concurred and offered her his arm.

The whole of their party relocated to Oakhurst Place for a celebratory breakfast, where it was discovered Gemma and Lady Bursbury had once more outdone themselves. There were various rolls, eggs done in every way imaginable, bacon, kippers, ham, pastries— anything any person could want, along with tea and hot chocolate.

"We may have been rather excessive," Gemma confessed.

"And I was just thinking we could have done with some strawberry jam as well," Lady Bursbury muttered.

His grandmother and Penelope's mother were elated at the union, their eyes practically glowing as they shared secret smiles between one another. As if silently congratulating each other on a match successfully made.

Before the food was consumed, MacKenzie and Penelope stood to receive their felicitations. There was a heartfelt hug from Gemma for each of them and allusion toward the expectation of great-grandchildren, an excited giggle from Lady Eugenia who was clearly already planning her own wedding and a wish of eternal good fortune from Kendal whom MacKenzie expected would slip away in a moment's time.

Lord Hesterton limped up and cast a bored expression at them. "Marriage is not at all what I expected," he drawled.

His wife, a pretty woman with dark hair, jabbed him lightly in the ribs. Their eyes met and they shared a soft laugh. "It's far, far better." He drew his wife toward him and pressed a kiss to her cheek.

"And I didn't make him say that," Lady Hesterton said. "Honestly. We hope you find as much joy with one another as we have." She took Penelope's hand and her smile widened. "I suspect you will."

Lord and Lady Hesterton shared a knowing look and moved on to take their seats.

"Oh, Penelope, you do look lovely." Lady Bursbury's eyes watered with emotion as she embraced her daughter.

"And we've a wedding present for you." Lord Bursbury grinned. "We're sending you on a wedding trip to Paris."

"Your rooms will overlook the Seine. And only for a week," Lady Bursbury rushed. "And not until at least next month so you may return to the hospital first." She reached for Penelope's hand. "We know how much it means to you, dear."

MacKenzie's lovely new wife beamed at her parents for the generous gift. It was an incredibly considerate gesture that showed in the way Penelope's eyes glowed.

Following all the well wishes came the great breakfast feast. MacKenzie and Penelope sat beside one another throughout the feast. Though he should not have been, he was aware of every movement she made, just as he noted the only thing that she ate out of all the proffered food was a couple of toast points and a bit of tea. Well, and a bite of the wedding cake, but then who did not eat wedding cake?

When at last it came time to bid farewell to their guests, they stood at the entryway and embraced each of their loved ones who had come to witness their vows. With each person who slipped away, one pressing question squeezed tighter and tighter at MacKenzie.

Now what?

What did one do with a new wife in their home? He could think of one particular activity he'd find preferable. However, it was one he ought to cross from his mind completely. But with an arrangement such as theirs, what *did* one do?

He supposed he would allow her time to become acclimated with her new surroundings and then share meals with one another. But outside of that...

"Everyone wishes us to be happy," Penelope said quietly at his side.

"I imagine our arrangement will please us both," MacKenzie said carefully. His eye caught something dangling from the ceiling just overhead. Was that mistletoe?

Gemma was the final guest to approach, walking now without the aid of a cane. The daily walks she took with Penelope had Gemma in better health than MacKenzie had ever seen her.

"Yes, my dear grandson." Her eye twinkled. "That is mistletoe and I'll not apologize for it."

Penelope turned her gaze up to regard the plant, her face unreadable.

MacKenzie cleared his throat. "It would appear we are expected to kiss."

"So it does." Penelope met his eyes and pressed her lips together. Her expression was no longer difficult to discern: she was nervous.

She had fine lips, full and heart shaped. As lovely as all the rest of her. Suddenly, MacKenzie found himself grateful for the mistletoe and the opportunity to sample her sweet mouth, but only if he could set his new wife at ease.

༄༅

PENELOPE'S HEARTBEAT ROARED IN HER EARS. *MISTLETOE*? HOW had she not seen it?

"Do ye know how the tradition of kissing under the mistletoe came to be?" Lord Oakhurst asked abruptly.

Penelope shook her head. "I do not. I do, however, know it can be used to assist with breathing difficulties and sometimes even quell fits of mania."

His stare lingered on her mouth as she spoke, and it made the pulse ticking at her wrist quicken.

"It was the Greeks," he said. "During Saturnalia, a festival of

Saturn performed before Christmas. The Romans used it as well and would resolve their disputes beneath the mistletoe."

Penelope regarded her new husband with a note of intrigue. "I wasn't aware of any of that."

He shrugged as though it were of little consequence. As though he had not just taught her something new. If there was anything Penelope loved even more than medicine, it was learning something new.

"There was a Nordic legend as well," he continued. "Frigga was the goddess of love. In a show of his usual mischief, the God, Loki, shot her son with an arrow made of mistletoe—a plant Frigga held sacred. She managed to save her son and declared henceforth anyone beneath mistletoe willna only be protected from death, but also deserving of a kiss."

Lord Oakhurst's jaw was smooth from a fresh shave. Unlike he had been the week before, when his jaw had been whiskered with a fine prickling of hair that made her want to run her sensitive palm over the bristles. The shadow of a beard had given him a fierce edge that she had grudgingly admitted she found rather appealing. Smooth or grizzled, her husband was a fine-looking man.

"I wasn't aware mistletoe had such a history." Penelope licked her lips and Lord Oakhurst's gaze slipped to her mouth once more.

There was a soft creak of the floorboards as his grandmother slipped from the room, leaving them completely alone. Husband and wife. Penelope's heartbeat tripped over itself and scrambled to catch up.

He glanced to where his grandmother had departed the room. "We dinna have to do this if ye dinna want to."

Kissing, Penelope knew, was often a prelude to sexual intercourse. And while he had agreed to no children, she knew he would want to consummate the marriage. For it to be truly legal and binding, of course.

She had done extensive research on what transpired between a man and woman and knew well what to expect. Lady Bursbury had attempted the conversation with her several days prior and had left with her hands over her ears declaring Penelope leave off with *such* details.

It was all just a physiological response to the introduction of arousal into one's system.

Arousal would effuse their bodies and make them change. He would become hard and she would become swollen and damp. Then he would fit inside her, like a hand sliding into a fitted glove. Or at least one finger of it. She had seen drawings.

Of course, in her time at the hospital, she had been the unmarried daughter of an earl and was barred from any dealings anywhere near the male genitalia. She realized now that it left her at a great disadvantage to be so lacking in knowledge on the topic of what would be, well, going inside of her.

She was just considering which finger the male organ might be —the thumb, presumably—when he delicately touched his fingertips to the underside of her chin and tilted her face upward. His moss-green eyes searched hers boldly in the intimacy of such closeness and a warmth pulsed between her legs.

Arousal, she noted clinically, did not take long to present itself.

"But if ye'd like to kiss, I wouldna decline." His mouth lifted in the playful smile she found boyishly charming.

Penelope had heard of women speak of their husband's blind fumbling in the marital bed. If Lord Oakhurst wished to kiss her first and allow arousal to heat her body first, she would gladly accept.

"We owe it to Frigga, do we not?" she replied softly.

His eyes crinkled at the corners with his smile. "Indeed." His hand glided from his hold on her chin to cradle her jaw, his touch light and tender. The mirth on his face melted to a focused seriousness that made her mouth suddenly go quite dry.

He lowered his head toward hers and she closed her eyes in anticipation for her first kiss. His lips met hers, far softer than she had anticipated. It was more than one kiss; their mouths closing against one another twice, then a teasing brush of his lips over hers, then one more kiss. It was foreign and tantalizing and over-whelmingly delightful.

It robbed her of her breath and left a curious tingling at her breasts.

He leaned back and restored the air his presence had stolen, so that she might once more breathe. She blinked her eyes open. Her mouth still tingled where his had touched hers and she tucked her lower lip into her mouth to savor it.

He studied her for a moment, doubtless ready to ask her to his chamber. She would go willingly, of course. Not because she was a wife, but because the power of arousal was far, far greater than she had given it credit for. She was weak-kneed with desire, her skin practically humming with heightened sensitivity. The light smoky scent of him, the sheer masculinity beneath, was altogether too appealing and made her want to breathe him in. She wanted more kisses to feed those lovely sensations until arousal overwhelmed them both.

Certainly, none of the books she had read discussed the grip of lust's control.

"Welcome to Oakhurst Place." Her husband stepped back a respectful distance. "The house is yers to do with as ye will. The library is well stocked, though I confess most are books on history." Again, that boyishly shy smile. "Ye may order whichever books ye like, anything really, through the housekeeper, Mrs. Stevens, who will assist ye with whatever else ye may require."

Penelope's mind reeled a moment. Was he not going to have her come to his chamber for consummation?

"Oh. Yes." Penelope's face heated with a furious blush. "Thank you."

"I shall stay out of yer way." He straightened his back, looking more of a regal earl than the man who had just kissed her so tenderly. "But am here should ye have need of me."

Penelope nodded. He nodded. And then it was done. He left. Just like that.

She stood for a moment of uncertainty as her body ran hot with the unspent arousal still pulsing through her.

It, unfortunately, did not dissipate as the day went on and she settled herself as much as one could in a new environment. Or rather, it would occasionally clear away until her mind inevitably wandered back to the recollection of that kiss.

Then her blood would grow hot and her breasts would feel heavy and that aching need would prevail between her thighs once more. It was terribly distracting. And she would be lying if she said she did not open several medical texts to revisit the draw-ings several times more, her curiosity renewed.

Lord Oakhurst did as he said he would. He left her to herself throughout the day. At supper that night, she saw him, as well as his grandmother. Their conversation had been light, focused on the wedding earlier that day, the upcoming wedding trip to Paris. Lord Oakhurst even brought up St. Thomas's, which was a consideration Penelope appreciated.

And yet through it all, her body remained agitated, raw with the unspent need simmering in her blood.

She'd gone to bed that night with anticipation humming in the air around her. Nighttime was when men came to their wives. The blind fumbling and all that.

Penelope had doused the candle and lay in wait. In fact, she lay in wait for a long time, wide awake, her gaze fixed on the door, her body craving a finish to what had been started.

At long last, a light showed under her door, shadowed by a pair of feet. Her breathing quickened at such a rapid rate, she nearly choked. She straightened in bed and self-consciously brushed her fingers over her hair to smooth any loose strands from her braid.

And then, as abruptly as the booted feet had appeared at her door, they were gone.

Penelope collapsed back into her bed and wondered at the possibility of expiring from the force of one's lust. She closed her eyes and willed sleep to come. When it did not, she did as she always had when sleep eluded her. She started at the bottom of the human skeleton and began to list the bones.

"Distal phalanges."

The way Lord Oakhurst had studied her before leaning down for the kiss.

"Intermediate phalanges."

How he had lowered toward her, his eyes closing.

"Proximal phalanges."

The softness of his lips.

"Metatarsals."

The smoothness of his chin.

She squeezed her eyes tight, suddenly fortunate for there being 206 bones in the human body. For she might have cause to recite every one of them that night.

⁂

MacKenzie splashed a finger of whisky into the cut crystal glass. A bit of it sloshed from the decanter and puddled on the polished surface of his desk.

Forgetting generally took eight glasses of whisky. At least that was what it had taken when his father died ten years prior. When Lady Judith and Gilbert had announced their engagement, its suddenness had required eight glasses.

MacKenzie lifted his ninth glass that evening. Even as it burned its way down his throat, he could not forget.

The way she had gazed up at him, with wide, innocent blue eyes.

Sip.

Flushed cheeks and lips. God, she had tasted sweet. Like the cake they had eaten. Like freshness and raw sensuality, a honey more enticing than he'd even known.

Sip.

Her skin had been so soft under his touch, as smooth as the porcelain it resembled.

Sip.

All of her would be that way.

Sip.

He curled his hand into a fist and clenched it with all the frustration roaring through him. He'd spew up the liquid sloshing in his stomach before his mind would relinquish those teasing thoughts. It was bloody hopeless.

She'd said she had no interest in lovers. Stated so simply, and with unquestioning assuredness. He knew well what that meant. No interest in carnal delights. A lack of desire to stay up through the wee hours of the morning, licking and tasting one another, rolling in the sheets until they were tangled and damp with sweat.

Nine glasses weren't enough to make him forget, but at least it had made his cock finally go soft. Thank heaven for small mercies.

He pushed himself up and the room tilted slightly. He gritted his teeth until the feeling passed and staggered from the room.

During his time in Scotland, he'd been on several boats. And on more than one occasion, they had hit rough seas. The elegant townhouse on Park Street suddenly left him feeling as though he were in turbulent waters now, aboard one of those rickety boats, knocking him about and leaving him reeling.

Even still, he knew her door when he passed it. He paused and stared, swaying with the nonexistent waves.

He'd stopped on the way to the library earlier too. But he hadn't knocked. Not when her room had been so silent and dark within. He knew the marriage for what it was: convenience. There was not sex with convenience.

Even if one's wife was the most beautiful woman in all of

London and Scotland, even when her kiss made his body burn like the blue center of a brilliant flame. Even when nine glasses of whisky could not make him forget how badly he wanted her.

He turned away from her door and made his way to his own chamber, to his own bed. The fire in his hearth did little to stave off the cold from the capacious chamber. He peeled back the bedding and lay down in his clothing without even bothering to slip off his boots.

As he waited for the world to stop swinging wildly about him, she entered his thoughts once more, and he knew with certainty that he should have made it ten whiskies.

🦋 7 🦋

The following morning did not find Penelope well rested. She had gone through all the bones in the body and then had started onto muscles before sleep finally claimed her. Even then, her slumber had been restless, fevered, peppered with pages of drawings of the male genitalia and how it fit inside that of a woman.

After dressing in a soft gown of white muslin and having her hair pulled back in a loose knot, she made her way down the elegant stairs to where breakfast would most likely be underway. She pushed the door open and stopped short.

Lord Oakhurst sat at the table with an odd-colored green drink in a crystal glass beside a cup of tea. He looked up from the paper he held and greeted her with a slow nod. Though he was dressed in a tailored waistcoat and shirt sleeves, he'd cast aside his coat and had opted not to shave. The result was intimate and altogether quite alluring.

Bashfulness twisted suddenly at her empty stomach. "Good morning."

"Good morning." There was a gravelly gruffness to his voice

that suggested he might have just woken recently. "I trust ye slept well."

"Yes, thank you," Penelope lied, but then added truthfully, "my chamber is lovely, and the bed is quite comfortable."

A light smile touched his lips. "Gemma will be glad to hear it. She spent the better part of this week traversing all over London, making sure everything she ordered would be just right for ye."

The Dowager Lady Oakhurst had clearly gone through tremendous effort to make Penelope feel welcome.

"That was very kind of her," Penelope said with sincerity. "Is she about? I'd like to see if I might join her in a walk later today."

"She should be down later," he replied.

Penelope slipped in the chair opposite him at the small table and found the most recent copy of *Medico-Chirurgical Transactions,* which was published by the Royal Medical and Chirurgical Society of London. Beside it was a plate with toast points and an empty teacup. She glanced to Lord Oakhurst.

He tilted his head at the periodical. "If ye prefer scandal sheets, my grandmother has a few of those fetched from time to time as well. And the kitchen can bring ye something else if ye prefer."

"This is perfect." Penelope pulled her plate closer to her. "Thank you for all of your considerations."

"I want ye to feel welcome." He lifted his glass of green liquid and drank it with a wince.

She couldn't help but give a small laugh. "What is that?"

"This?" He scowled at the drink. "It's a concoction created by Lord Kendal to take the edge off a night of drinking."

Penelope's face went hot in spite of herself. Lord Oakhurst must have gone out after she was in bed. After he'd paused in front of her door. She was not ignorant to the activities of men and where their proclivities lay. Not that any of it should be her concern, she reminded herself. If he found himself in the arms of a doxy or a mistress, it would be of little consequence to her.

It had to be.

Except that he had not taken the time to consummate the marriage with her first. She had been burning with desire in that large bed while he had been cavorting.

"I hope it was enjoyable," she murmured.

"It wasna one of my better nights." He lifted *The Times* and fixed his attention on the small print.

Gambling then. Not women. Her shoulders relaxed.

Silence descended on the room and left Penelope with the feeling that she ought to fill the space with something. Anything.

She shifted in her chair and glanced at him. He was looking at the paper, distracted, not noticing as she let her gaze wander over his face, his mouth. She pressed her lips together as the fresh wave of memories rolled back along with the familiar, agonizing throb of arousal.

Abruptly, he set aside the paper and regarded her with raised brows. "I know what ye're thinking."

Penelope's cheeks blazed. "Do you?" she asked, hoping her expression did not reveal the entirety of her mortified horror.

"The ball," he replied.

The ball? What ball?

She opened her mouth to speak but closed it with uncertainty.

"Perhaps ye were thinking of something else then." He pushed at the stubborn lock at his forehead that curled back into place, thankfully not guessing as to where her thoughts might have strayed.

"I meant yer parent's ball," he continued.

"Yes." She touched her brow at her own forgetfulness. Lady Bursbury had planned her ball for the day after their wedding. She'd sworn it had "absolutely nothing" to do with Penelope and Lord Oakhurst's marriage, but Penelope knew her mother better than to believe such an outlandish claim or such a timely coincidence. "That's this evening, isn't it?"

He nodded.

A servant entered with a fresh pot of tea and poured them each a cup. The sweet, floral scent pulled her in. She grasped the cup and brought it to her lips. It was just cool enough to prevent her from scalding her tongue: the ideal temperature.

She sighed softly. "I'll be ready at half past seven."

He drank a sip of tea and held the teacup in his hands after. "I'll save a dance for ye if ye save one for me."

"Misery does love company." Penelope sipped at her tea again as Lord Oakhurst chuckled into his cup.

Penelope had always detested dancing. Being so close to another person, sharing the same air, had never held appeal.

Until now.

She tried to recall the dance with Lord Oakhurst previously, but the memory blurred with the many other men she'd danced with that night. Tonight, she knew, would be different. She wanted to be close to him, to share the same air, the same space, to breathe him in.

Frustration tightened through her. This was ridiculous. She was a grown woman, one who had fought her way in to establish a foothold in the world of medicine. If she wanted something, she knew well how to get it.

"Dare I ask what ye're thinking now?" he asked. His Scottish burr was like a sensual whisper to her senses, caressing her ears and sending prickles of anticipation tingling through her.

Penelope considered his question. How did one ask for their marriage to be consummated? Surely it would be brazen to speak so plainly, perhaps too bold. Unless, of course, she expressed a desire to follow the general rules of marriage. Yes, that would be the best route to go.

"What I was thinking was...well, I'm afraid it's rather pedantic," she began.

"Pedantic?" He lifted his teacup to his mouth.

"Yes." She folded her hands demurely in her lap and regarded him from across the table. "I should like to have our marriage consummated."

THE TEA MACKENZIE HAD BEEN DRINKING CAUGHT FAST IN HIS throat and sputtered from between his lips, staining the white tablecloth.

He straightened, set his teacup aside and wiped at his mouth. "I beg your pardon?"

She met his incredulous stare. "I should like to consummate our marriage."

He swallowed. "Now?"

She flushed and glanced shyly around the room. "Is it done in the light of day?" she asked. "And outside of the bedchamber?"

"It certainly can be," he murmured.

"I'm sorry?" She raised her brows in silent question.

"We can go to the bedchamber if you like." He adjusted his waistcoat, grateful he'd discarded his jacket. One less bit of clothing to have to remove. It was only morning and Kendal's hangover cure hadn't fully done its magic yet, but he could perform. His groin twitched with anticipation. Oh yes, he'd have no problem performing.

Her rosy cheeks made his imagination go wild. He wanted to bring on more of those blushes, until the fair skin of her neck and chest were pink.

She bit her lower lip. "I think this evening would be more proper."

He balled his hand into a fist under the table and squeezed it to regain control of the smack of lust pummeling his brain. A man should not want his wife this badly.

"Aye, of course." He nodded.

"After the ball," she added.

Damn the bloody ball. Never had he hated a social event with such ferocity. He wanted to enjoy the entire night with her, carefully divesting her of her clothing one silky, lacy bit at a time. He wanted to taste and tease her until she was crying out with need. He wanted—

"I confess," she whispered. "I wish we were not attending the ball tonight. I am..."

He remained perfectly still, poised for her last word, waiting to hear exactly what might follow.

"Curious," she said quietly.

Did she mean for her voice to be so low and sensual? It glided over him like a caress. He squeezed his fist again. Good God.

"Curious?" he repeated.

"Yes." Her fingertip gracefully traced the curled handle of the teacup. "After our kiss yesterday, I found myself quite aroused."

If MacKenzie had been drinking tea, it would have sprayed over the tablecloth a second time.

He pushed the cup away, resolved not to have a single sip until their discussion was complete. Hopefully in his bedchamber with her wearing nothing but one of her beautiful blushes.

The maid entered at that exact moment and the conversation between them dropped away. She placed a small tray of pastries on the table and her gaze fell on the stained tablecloth.

MacKenzie waved his hand for her to ignore it. She bobbed a quick curtsey, refilled their tea at a painfully slow pace, then finally slipped from the room.

"Is it terribly wicked to say what I've said to you?" Lady Penelope asked. "It is, isn't it?"

It was just the right amount of wicked, but he'd never say as much.

"I'm yer husband, lass." He settled back into his chair with a feigned ease. "Ye can tell me anything."

She nodded and pressed her lips together as though trying to deduce where to start.

Please continue with talk of arousal. He would make breakfast last a whole bloody day if this was where their talk veered.

"Will you kiss me again?" she asked.

God, she was audacious, and he loved it. "Now?" he asked. "In the light of day? And outside the bedchamber?" He winked at her.

She laughed at that, her eyes shining. Audacious and beautiful. And she wanted him.

She wanted their naked skin against one another.

She wanted his touch, his hands, his *mouth*, on her body.

She wanted his cock *inside* of her. And God, did he wish it to be there.

Of course, she hadn't said those words exactly, but he was a man, and that was precisely what he'd heard.

"Now would be amenable." Her boldness melted to just the right amount of reticence and MacKenzie thought his heart might thump out of his chest. He rose and offered her his hand, as though inviting her for a dance. She put her fingers to his palm and got to her feet.

Her hand was cool against the heat of his, a wonderful contrast.

She faced him with shy expectation. He let go of her hand and stroked her cheek before gently cupping her jaw. She swallowed and looked up at him.

His thumb brushed her bottom lip and her quiet gasp whispered over the digit. He lowered his face toward hers and her lashes swept over her cheeks as she closed her eyes. If their previous kiss had resulted in her arousal, he would ensure this one made the seconds between now and after the ball drag on for all eternity.

His mouth moved over hers in a tender kiss that she returned with innocent eagerness. She leaned into him, welcoming his kiss. Impatient for it.

For him.

He slid his hand to the back of her head. Her hair was like the finest silk, smooth against his fingertips. He caught her bottom lip in his mouth and sucked ever so gently.

A little moan sounded in the back of her throat.

God.

His tongue teased lightly against her lips and she opened for him, letting him sweep inside her mouth. She tasted sweet, of tea and the bit of sugar she'd put into it. Her moan was louder this time.

MacKenzie threaded his fingers into her glossy hair and deepened the kiss. Her hand came to his chest and rested upon him like a brand as her tongue met his. Her curious tongue probed at his before stroking with confidence and desire.

Desire.

If he'd meant to encourage her into lust, he was about to burn himself to ash in the effort. His veins were alighting with fire, every part of him completely in tune with her, his skin crackling with awareness. If she weren't a virgin, he might clear their breakfast from the table with one sweep of his arm and take her right where they'd been having tea only moments before.

But now was for tantalizing. Enticing.

His free hand went to her waist as his tongue tangled with hers. Slowly, carefully, he slid his fingers up to her breasts. She pushed into his touch, encouraging him. Her nipples were taut beneath the soft muslin. He brushed his thumb over one and she whimpered with need.

He loved a woman with sensitive breasts. It allowed him the opportunity to enjoy them, kissing and suckling the pink buds. He longed to do that now.

Before he realized what he was doing, his mouth was trailing down her slender, graceful neck, licking and nipping a path to her neckline. His tongue edged the fine fabric as his fingers worked at it, tugging it down so the swell of one fair breast came into view.

He wanted more. *Needed* more.

Penelope issued forth a breathy moan that damn near sent

him to the wrong side of sanity. He pressed his thumb at the center of her breast and a rosy nipple popped free of its stays. He groaned and closed his mouth around it, flicking his tongue against the hardened little nub.

Penelope moaned with audible delight. MacKenzie had always loved a woman who let him know she enjoyed his efforts. Penelope was a woman who would let him know with every sigh and moan.

"Oh." She clung to the back of his head, locking him against her. "Lord Oakhurst."

Lord Oakhurst. It would be almost funny if he weren't so damn aroused. His cock throbbed, practically aching with need. For her. He needed her. Too much.

It was time to stop or he might have difficulty doing so.

He gave her nipple a final, sensual lick, then straightened as he tucked her fine breast back into place. "Call me MacKenzie, lass."

Her cheeks were scarlet, and her neck and chest were flushed pink. Exactly as he'd expected. Her lids were heavy, and her eyes sparkled with yearning.

"MacKenzie?" she said in a breathy voice.

He had to fight the urge to draw her into his arms again and finish what they'd started.

"No." She tilted her head. "That's our surname. And I'm not one of your university chums. I'm your wife, even if only for convenience."

"And curiosity," he added with a grin.

Her gaze slid down to where his cock strained against the placket of his breeches. She smiled; a sensual curl of her lips that made him even harder. "James," she said.

He'd never liked his English name and had always found it rather off-putting. That is, until she said it. In that seductive purr. *James.* The way she spoke made him want her lips at his ear, moaning his name.

With all the control he could muster, he offered a respectful bow and backed away. "I shall leave ye to yer day." He straightened with a grin. "Until tonight."

8

Drawn out.
        Unending.
Ceaseless.
Interminable.

There were many words that Penelope knew could describe something that felt as if it was dragging on forever, and yet not a one of them truly defined the time that stretched from morning until the evening of the ball. It was as though a lifetime had passed since that kiss.

That kiss.

Could something so delightful, so intimate, be referred to simply as a kiss?

She doubted it. The way he'd eased her breast from her stays and licked her—

Footsteps sounded behind her. She spun around, aware of how her cheeks blazed. Lord Oakhurst stood there in a black tailcoat with tan pantaloons and a champagne-colored cravat with the gold "W" pin he wore glinting at the silken center.

He'd combed his hair neatly back with that one stubborn curl at his brow. The strangest urge to run her fingers through his hair to brush it back nearly overcame her.

It was then she realized Lord Oakhurst was staring at her.

No, not Lord Oakhurst.

James.

The very thought of his name sent a small shiver down her spine.

"Ye look...stunning." He closed the distance between them, his moss-green eyes deepening in such a way, it made her blood go hot and her thoughts turn wicked.

His chin was smooth again, having evidently been scraped free of all bristles for the ball.

The way it had been when they'd kissed the first time. Not like that morning, when the prickle of his whiskers had rasped against her chin...and her breast.

Oh, heavens.

She looked down at her gown, desperate to break eye contact, lest he see directly into her salacious thoughts.

Her mother had ordered the white silk gown specifically for the "winter ball" she was hosting. A thin netting of tissue lay over the gown like a veil and sparkled with dozens of tiny gemstones. Similar gemstones were clustered around a small bunch of curling white feathers that had been fastened into her hair at the nape of her neck, nestled within pinned curls.

Did all husbands compliment their wives so? Penelope knew her father often flattered Lady Bursbury. But husbands who were simply acquired through marriage as an act of convenience, surely, they did not.

It seemed...unnecessary.

"You look quite handsome." She spoke not to repay the compliment out of politeness, but in truth. He did look handsome.

In fact, he piqued her carnal curiosity all the more. She

wondered at what he looked like beneath the broad-shouldered tailcoat and pressed shirt, beneath his pantaloons.

She glanced around the room. "Will your grandmother be joining us?"

"She's already at Bursbury Place, assisting Lady Bursbury with the supervision of any final necessary preparations." He offered her his arm and the woodsy scent of him embraced her awareness and made her skin hum. "Shall we?"

Penelope rested her hand in the warm crook of his arm and allowed him to lead her into the carriage. This marked the first time in her adult life she had been enclosed in the quiet intimacy of a carriage alone with a man who was not her father. And not just any man, but the one she planned to have intercourse with upon their return to Oakhurst Place. The man who had left her body burning with the advanced stages of arousal for the duration of a night and a day.

He allowed her to climb into the carriage first and then sat on the seat across from her. Lights from outside flickered over his face as they made the journey to her former home.

Silence descended between them, tense and thick. Not with discomfort, but with lust.

The corners of his lips quirked upward. "Ye're staring, Lady Oakhurst."

"So are you, Lord Oakhurst," she replied.

"I want to kiss ye." He lifted his chin, regal and debonair as he made the sinful statement with tantalizing nonchalance.

"Here?" she asked, far more tempted than she cared to admit.

He leaned forward, bracing his elbows on his knees and for one heart-fluttering moment, she thought he might make good on his wish. Instead his fingers grazed against hers where they rested on her knee.

Arousal hummed in her veins like liquid fire.

"Tonight, after the ball," he promised with the burr of his Scottish accent. He brushed her hand with his. "Then here." His fingertips whispered over her knee and teased an inch up her thigh. "And here."

Penelope's mouth went dry even as other areas of her body became, well...rather wet.

The carriage rolled to a stop. He straightened as smoothly as he'd leaned forward and the door snapped open. Icy air swept into the carriage, but even the frigid temperature was not enough to cool her cheeks.

They climbed out and James offered her his arm. This time, taking it held an intimacy, a crackling connection between them as she sensed the strength of his forearm beneath his sleeve. They walked in together, Penelope's cheeks aflame with lust, and immediately became the center of attention as the caller announced them by their newly married titles of the Earl and Countess of Oakhurst.

Penelope endured the press of all those stares with a pleasant smile expertly applied to her lips. James settled his free hand over her arm. To most in the room, it might look like a show of possession, but she caught sight of the glance he gave her. Understanding.

He understood her unease and sought to comfort her.

Once the attention finally faded away, she was left to join the ladies who were eagerly awaiting her company, just as a cluster of men clearly waited on him. At least without James at her side, Penelope would be able to breathe again. Think again.

He stole all her senses when he was near. Consumed them. Held them with rapt need.

"I would like yer first dance," he said in a low voice. "Before the other men try to steal ye away."

Penelope chuckled. The men of the ton had given up on her long ago. She was too odd a young woman, her passion for medicine confusing and strange and entirely off-putting. "I'm sure you've nothing to worry about."

His gaze flicked down her body. It was quick enough that

others most likely would not notice, but it blazed with an intent that scorched through her. "I'm sure I do."

Her pulse quickened. "Very well, but only the first set. The others, I shall have to beat men back with lengthy dissertations on the art of medicine. I've found that works rather well."

His mouth eased into a relaxed smile and it struck her again how handsome he was. "Save yer speech on gout for me."

"Only the best for you." She tossed him a coy smile and with that, she swept away toward her mother and sister, who stood with James's grandmother.

"Darling, you look so happy." Lady Bursbury embraced Penelope and enveloped her in the sweet, powdery scent she'd always associated with her mother. "And lovely. That gown suits you so very well. I do hope you've been enjoying my presents." Her mother tilted her head and smiled in such a way that made Penelope immediately wary.

"I helped with their placement," the Dowager Lady Oakhurst said with a twinkle in her eye.

Their...placement?

"The gown is lovely," Penelope said slowly.

"Oh." Lady Bursbury shared a conspiratorial glance with James's grandmother. "Yes, well, there are several more presents. I supposed you will find them in good time."

Eugenia grabbed Penelope's hand before she could ask more. "When I am wed," Eugenia confided in a soft voice, "I want my husband to look at me as Lord Oakhurst looks at you now."

Penelope opened her mouth to protest even as she glanced across the room. She immediately located James without effort and discovered he was indeed staring at her. He didn't look away when he realized he'd been caught, but instead offered her a cocky half grin and returned his attention to Lord Kendal.

There was an arrogance in that grin, one she'd always hated in others. And yet in James, she found it—as she found a surprising number of things with him—appealing.

But then, she was beginning to learn James was not like other men of the ton.

❦

MacKenzie let his gaze slip back to Penelope the moment she wasn't looking. He'd never enjoyed attending balls, or any English social function for that matter. Anywhere that his Scottish accent made him stand out like—a smile pulled at his lips— like a gouty toe.

"I presume marriage is treating you kindly," Kendal drawled.

The earl watched MacKenzie with a bemused expression. He pushed a brandy into MacKenzie's empty hand.

MacKenzie accepted the drink with thanks. "Why do ye say that?"

"I dare say you were smiling just now," Kendal offered dryly. "That, and the way your new wife is looking at you at this very moment."

MacKenzie's stare flicked back in her direction to find her watching him. She flushed in the lovely way she did and quickly turned away, leaving Kendal chortling into his glass of brandy.

"How did you do it?" Kendal asked with a raised brow. "When she first came out, I think every man in London sought to court her at some point. Except me, of course." He lifted the corners of his mouth roguishly.

Dancers were beginning to gather on the dance floor for the opening set, the one Penelope had promised to him. "I promised not to love her."

He pushed his glass back into Kendal's free hand and ignored his friend's confused look as he sought out Penelope. She was standing beside her mother and Gemma, both of whom wore gleeful expressions.

. . .

"THE FIRST DANCE WILL BE THE WALTZ," LADY BURSBURY practically sang out her announcement to him.

Of course, it would be the waltz.

He offered his arm to Penelope and led her to the dance floor.

"I apologize for my mother," she said softly.

"And I apologize for my grandmother." He took Penelope in his arms for the start of the dance. "I also apologize for how badly I want this ball to be over."

The music began and soared over the hum of conversation.

"Don't," Penelope said softly. "At least not to me. I want it to be over too."

She was petite and graceful in his arms, pressed close to his body, as he managed his way around the ballroom. It was hard not to let his hands linger too long when he wanted to skim his palms over the various intriguing parts of her body.

His blood ran hotter than it ever had during a dance and, much to his great discomfort, his cock began responding to Penelope's nearness. He gazed down into her wide blue eyes and kept himself from glancing at her lips.

"Talk to me about gout," he said through gritted teeth.

"Is your grandmother's toe bothering her again?" Concern puckered at Penelope's brow.

"I am...in terrible need of distraction." He spun her in front of him, grateful for the way she blocked his body with her own as he did so. Once she was in front of him once more, he spoke quietly into her ear. "In yer words, I've found myself quite aroused."

"Oh." The word purred from her in a way that certainly did not help matters.

He held her closer as they twirled together. Their pelvises met briefly, and he caught her soft intake of breath. "Oh," she repeated again, clearly feeling him pressed to her.

"That isna helping," he said in a droll tone.

She laughed, though the comment had been offered without amusement.

"Gout," he demanded.

"Very well." She smiled up at him, spun around for the dance and said, "The initial stages appear on the foot with reddened, inflamed skin around the metatarsal-phalangeal joint of the large toe."

He nodded. "Keep going."

"The pain stems from crystals growing under the skin in the form of sharp spikes," she continued.

He almost missed a step. "Good God."

"Is this helping?" she asked with a coy smile.

"Aye, so long as ye dinna keep looking at me like that." He led her through the dance, his body no longer hard, what with thoughts of sharp crystals forming inside a foot. And how terribly it must hurt poor Gemma.

"I want to know more too," she said.

"About gout?" He raised a brow.

"About your particular interests."

He quirked an eyebrow at her. "History."

"Do tell me more." Did she have to give him such a coquettish smile?

History. Now there was a topic he could use his mind for rather than imagining Penelope stripped naked and in his arms with pink-tipped breasts and—

"Greek history especially," he said with determination. "I enjoy that most of all."

"I should like to hear more." Her cheeks reddened. "I find I too am—"

"No. Dinna say it."

She laughed again, a sweet sound he wouldn't mind hearing more of.

"Did ye know the word 'idiot' had its origins in ancient Greece?" He lifted a brow.

Her eyes twinkled in a rather becoming manner. "I did not."

"It referred to someone who dinna bother with politics."

They both had a good chuckle at that. Thanks to the discussion of history and gout, they made it through the waltz. In fact, discussions of apoplexy, dropsy, Greek mythology and of course, the Elgin Marbles carried them into a lively country dance later that evening and even a supper with far too many courses.

In preventing the burn of lust from scorching his veins, MacKenzie realized he'd learned quite a bit about the medical field in which Penelope had devoted so much of her life. And that she seemed genuinely interested in what he knew of history.

After they had eaten, Gemma approached him, her face weary. "Forgive me, James, but I fear I can't stay up as late as I once did. The two of you can remain longer, of course. I'll send the carriage back round—"

"No," both MacKenzie and Penelope answered at once.

"That isn't necessary," Penelope quickly added. "I expect to get a reply from Dr. Cooper sometime tomorrow, welcoming me back to St. Thomas's. I ought to get a good amount of rest in anticipation of such a busy day."

MacKenzie sent his man to go collect the carriage. "And I've got a letter from Mr. Barclay to attend to, as well as a meeting with parliamentary session I cannot miss tomorrow."

"Ah." Gemma nodded and gave them a look that was more knowing than anyone ever wanted to receive from their grandmother.

Lady Bursbury was not at all disappointed at their early departure either, most likely expecting it, given Penelope's dislike for social events. Except that she too had a glint in her eye.

It was enough to drive a man to distraction, were he not already incredibly, wonderfully distracted. Especially when the carriage arrived more swiftly than anticipated, delivered them home without issue and Gemma promptly bid them both goodnight without preamble.

And finally, they were left completely, blissfully alone.

❧ 9 ❧

Penelope's whole being flooded with nervous excitement as she met James's eyes.

He had loosened his cravat, revealing the muscles of his neck beneath. "Shall we retire, Lady Oakhurst?" he asked, his voice silky with implication.

"Yes," she breathed.

He stared at her for a long moment as though he meant to kiss her where she stood. Instead, he offered her his arm, which she accepted with a trembling hand. Together they made their way up the stairs, formal and without speaking. Every part of Penelope hummed with energy, with anticipation and raw, primal need.

Once they reached the landing, she hesitated, uncertain if they ought to go to his chamber or hers. She hadn't bothered to ask about the etiquette of such things but had advised her maid she would not require her assistance that evening, regardless. In the end, Penelope let him lead her in the direction of her own chamber.

With the immaculate manners of a gentleman, James opened

the door to her room and allowed her to enter before him. But when he closed the door behind him, formality ended.

"Penelope." He groaned her name with his wonderful brogue and pulled her into his arms.

Their mouths clashed against one another's in a desperate, frantic kiss that only served to flood more arousal into Penelope's system. James's hands went to her body, moving over her, feeling her through the lovely white gown, and he was not the only one touching.

Penelope ran her fingers over his chest and boldly skimmed over his torso, learning his shape from beneath the superfine wool of his coat and the silk of his green waistcoat. His heartbeat thundered in wild, pounding beats that matched hers as it roared in her ears.

"I want ye so bloody bad," he growled into her mouth.

She wanted to reply in kind, to tell him how she'd spent the entire day dying for this moment to arrive. Except at that exact moment, he eased his thigh between hers, grinding their bodies together. Friction—delightful, exquisite friction—teased at her core, easing the ache as much as encouraging it. If her mind were not so taken with lust, she might have pondered over her curious response more.

Except with James, there was not room for thought. Not in moments such as this.

He gripped her gown with his hand, slowly lifting the hem to reveal first her stockings, then her pale thighs showing just above them. His fingertips brushed the inside of her knee, where he'd touched her in the carriage. Penelope kept her attention fixed intensely on him, wanting the sweep of his fingers to shift higher, to the place that burned with need.

He did not disappoint.

Higher and higher he worked his fingers, until Penelope thought she might die from wanting. At long last, his caress brushed over the intimate, intensely sensitive place between her legs. Her legs buckled at first contact.

James grinned as he caught her and held her upright. "Do ye like that?" he whispered.

She nodded, not daring to trust herself to speak.

"Do ye want more of it?"

She nodded again, emphatically this time.

He chuckled and his hand moved over her once more, another wave of euphoria rolling through her. On and on he went, gliding over her wetness, encouraging her arousal further. Merciful heavens, probing inside of her with his finger and touching the apex of her sex where the small bud was swollen and desperate for attention.

Just when she thought she might actually explode, he withdrew his hand. Her skirt fell back into place and she whimpered her disappointment. His mouth found hers, kissing her deeply, almost aggressive with passion. He worked at the back of her dress, blindly undoing the small buttons as she shoved his tailcoat to the ground and made her own progress with the buttons of his waistcoat.

Clothing was untied, unbuttoned, unlaced and pushed aside with eagerness until there was only her shift and his pantaloons and shirt remaining. He tugged his shirt over his head, revealing a body carved with muscle. A light dusting of black hair sprinkled over his chest and a trail of it disappeared into the waistline of his pants.

She returned her gaze to his torso once more, taking all of him in. He was beautiful. Powerful. Her hands itched to run over the cut lines of his torso and glide her fingers down that enticing line of hair on his banded lower stomach. Their breathing was heavy and filled the silence of the room, a sound she never would have realized would be so intimate.

"I want to see ye with yer hair down," he said in that low, sensual tone.

It was such an unexpected and simple request that Penelope's hands immediately went to her hair and pulled first the dainty bundle of gems and feathers, then slipped the pins free. She gathered them in her palm until there were too many to hold and let them slip to the ground with tinkling plinks and plops. The coiled curls fell around her shoulders and the sweet perfume of her rose water emanated from her auburn waves.

James groaned and combed his hands through her tresses. She closed her eyes against the pleasure of it, reveling in the tingles across her scalp. He breathed in deep, as though savoring the scent of her.

"I want to see all of ye," he said on an exhale in her ear. His breath was spicy and alluring as it caressed the delicate skin of her neck. "Penelope."

Her heartbeat thrummed a little faster at the manner in which he said her name. She lifted the edge of her shift and drew it over her head.

James uttered a curse. She slowly elevated her gaze up to him, shy despite the force of her longing. He stared at her unabashedly, lust evident in the brightness of his eyes.

She reached for the fastenings of his fall and undid them. His erection sprang out at only three loosened buttons. The thing was bigger than large. It was massive.

She gasped in shock. "I thought..."

He lifted his brows.

"I thought it would be the size of a thumb," she admitted weakly.

He smirked. "I daresay that's rather insulting."

"But it's not." Penelope gaped at the thing. "It's enormous." Of course, she knew a woman's opening was made to allow for a babe to pass through, but goodness! She had not anticipated a man's organ could swell to such proportions.

"Well now, that's better." He grinned, an arrogant quirk of his lips and undid the rest of his buttons before pushing his pants from his waist. He pulled her into his arms, naked skin against naked skin. The thickness of his considerable organ rested heavy and hot against her stomach.

James held her face in his hands and kissed her, tender and chaste at first, then stroking her tongue with his, deepening the kiss until she was panting with desire once more.

He took her hand and guided it toward his enormous erection. She did not draw away, especially not when his own fingers went back to her sex. If his ministrations made her senses unfurl, doubtless her own attempts would feel equally as blissful on him. She ran her hand over his shaft. It was hard as though it contained a bone, which she knew it did not, but the skin was silky and hot and altogether far too tantalizing.

He gave a shuddering breath.

"Do you like that?" she whispered as he'd done with her.

He smiled between their kisses. "Ach, aye."

With his free hand, he curled her hand around him. The tick of his pulse was powerful there as his penis practically leapt with each beat of his heart. She slid over him until she reached the tip, which had a bulbous head that was decidedly less firm than the shaft, almost spongy. Her fingers worked over it in exploration and he groaned low and deep.

Fascinating.

He eased a finger inside of her at that exact moment and found the bud of her sex with the heel of his hand. All musings came to a crashing halt in her mind as lust prevailed and her hips bucked reflexively toward his hand.

He withdrew his touch once more and swept her into his arms. She gasped in surprise, which made him grin as he carried her to the bed and lay her upon it. Her heart thundered in her chest, wild with excitement...and a note of consternation.

He climbed onto the bed and hovered over her, naked, the heat of his manhood laying against her stomach. As if sensing her virginal hesitation, he kissed her again and slipped a finger inside her. With gentle care, he moved the digit in and out, tenderly stretching and teasing until she writhed on the bed, wanting more, needing him to touch that bud between her legs again. All her focus was on the gradual build of pleasure, so that she scarcely noticed him crawling lower, spreading her thighs further apart, his head lowering.

He leaned closer to her sex and parted his lips, but it was far too late to stop him as he looked up at her and licked her center. Any mortification she might have felt was singed away by the intensity of the euphoria as his tongue circled the sensitive bud of her sex. He lapped at her with vigor and she shamelessly spread her legs wide to welcome his ministrations.

Her body was alighting with need, for this. For him.

MACKENZIE COULD SENSE WHEN PENELOPE WAS NEARING climax from the hitch of her breath and the tightening of her core. Not yet. Not now. He drifted away from her despite her whimper of protest. God, how he wanted her to whimper like that every time he drew away from her.

He stretched over her, loving the sensation of her beneath him. She was lithe, but not without curves. He trailed his hand down her narrow waist to where her hips flared out and cupped her bottom. This was the part he was anticipating as much as dreading.

It was one thing to pleasure a woman. It was quite another to take her maidenhead. Or so he'd heard. It was why he'd held off on giving her relief for so long, in the hopes she might be distracted enough with desire to not feel as much of the initial discomfort.

He edged himself between her legs, careful to keep his weight elevated off of her. Good God, he was so hard with lust, it actually pained him.

Penelope watched him through heavy lidded eyes. A flush covered her cheeks, neck and lovely chest. Exactly as James had anticipated it would. It left her lips and skin rosy, as well as her nipples. He caught one between his lips for good measure and swirled it with his tongue.

She cried out in delight and he angled his cock toward her entrance. She was wet, glistening with the effects of her longing.

He'd made certain of that. Wet and hot and beyond ready. His prick ached to thrust into the root inside her, to stroke himself to completion.

He replaced his mouth with his hand on her breast and kissed her as he gently nudged inside her until he felt the slight resistance of a barrier. She moaned against his lips and arched her hips to encourage his entry. He swept his thumb over her nipple and pushed into her more.

Her eyes went wide.

He tensed, freezing over her. "Are ye all right?"

She nodded. "It was my hymen," she said tightly. "I knew it would happen."

"I think it will feel better as we go," MacKenzie offered, however helpful or unhelpful his words were.

She nodded.

He proceeded, one cautious inch at a time as he withdrew and entered her once more, this time slightly deeper than the last. He released her breast and moved his fingers between them, finding the little nub where a woman's pleasure centered, and rubbed it with small circles.

Her breath caught again, and she relaxed under him. Devil take it, she felt good. *Damn* good. Tight and sweet where she gripped him inside her as he stroked into her, taking her in slow, careful thrusts.

"Is that better?" he asked.

Her lashes fluttered and she nodded with a breathy exhale. Her hands roamed over his back as she held him more tightly, melding her body closer to his. Her hips rolled in time with his, encouraging his pace, getting him to pump harder, quicker.

Each arch on her part made her core clench around him, bringing on a tightening of his bollocks. Her panting came at a higher pitch and her sex tensed.

He flicked his finger faster over her bud, knowing how close she was to climax, and sending her over the edge. She came hard with a scream she buried into his shoulder.

Her core squeezed rhythmically around him, taking him with her into a powerful orgasm. He withdrew quickly from her, took his cock in fist, and pumped it hard thrice before spilling his seed into his other hand.

Penelope opened her eyes and looked up at him with understanding. There would be no child conceived from their joining.

"Thank you," she said softly.

He climbed from the bed and went to the ewer. "There used to be a plant in ancient Greece called silphium that prevented a woman from conceiving," he offered as he cleaned himself. "Except that it was in such high demand, they extinguished the plant from existence." He wet a bit of linen and carried it back to the bed for her.

She took it shyly with another word of thanks and wiped her virgin's blood from between her thighs.

"I hope that wasna too uncomfortable." He rubbed at a tense spot at the back of his neck.

She bit her lip and shook her head. "Only in the beginning. I was expecting it."

"The next time willna be painful, as I understand it." He took the cloth from her. "Would you like me to fetch ye a clean chemise?"

She smiled. "Please."

He went to the wardrobe, opened the wooden doors and reached in to grab a white linen shift. Except it was no ordinary shift that unfolded from his hands. The thing was made of wispy white lace, so delicate a man would be able to see straight through it. With so many holes, he could lick…

"What is that?" Penelope asked, her mouth falling open in apparent horror.

"I was about to ask ye that verra question." MacKenzie adjusted his grip to hold it up fully for his perusal. Yes, her pink nipples would be evident through the material, as would the red downy curls between her legs. She would be glorious in such a gown, with her fiery hair spilling over her shoulders.

"That isn't mine," she gasped.

"Is it no'?" He didn't lower it. "It appears to be exactly yer size."

"It's nothing I've ever seen before."

"That makes two of us." He held it out with a grin. "Ye should try it on to make certain."

She shook her head and the flush at her cheeks deepened. He didn't want to make her uncomfortable, not after what they'd just shared—especially when he hoped they would do it again in the future. He carefully folded the gown—if such a thing could be called a gown—and retrieved a chemise of linen from her wardrobe.

She climbed out of bed, beautifully naked, and pulled it on. It was a pity seeing a lovely body of creamy skin and firm breasts fall beneath a blanket of cloth in such a manner. He slid into her bed and waited for her. It was a foolish idea to consider sleeping the night with her, he knew. But it felt so strange to take a woman's virginity and then promptly leave once pleasure had been sated. She was not a lady of the night; she was his wife.

She regarded him curiously but joined him beneath the covers regardless. She shifted slightly and set her icy toes against him. Lucky for her, MacKenzie was often overwarm and always looking for a reprieve from his own internal heat.

"Ye're freezing." He caught her and pulled her against him.

Her chilled limbs settled against him, pleasantly cooling his body.

"That isn't—" She sighed with apparent contentment. "That does feel quite nice. I don't want to make you cold."

"I'm no' ever cold." He secured an arm around her shoulder and she cuddled against him.

"And I'm seldom ever hot." Her head shifted on his shoulder so she could look at him. "What brought about your fascination with history?"

"My da." MacKenzie smiled to himself. "We lived in Scotland until I was around ten, then we came back to England. In that time, I'd picked up this accent that's so popular with the ton." He paused to give an exaggerated smirk. "I dinna get on well with my classmates. Or rather, they dinna get on well with me."

"There's more to life than being accepted by society," Penelope said with a hint of bitterness.

"Tell that to my younger self." MacKenzie looped a lock Penelope's hair around his finger. "My da saw how miserable I was and showed me all the fascinating things my history teachers had left out."

"Why did you leave Scotland?" she asked.

He paused before answering, hating how raw the reply still was after all these years. "Death," he said simply. "My ma died when I was ten. It's why we left her home country to return to where my da had been raised."

"And why did you then leave England later?"

He hesitated. "Yer full of questions."

She smiled. "I'm a curious woman."

"Aye." He traced a fingertip over her naked shoulder. "I like that about ye."

She watched him with expectation, clearly waiting on an answer.

"I told ye I dinna want to marry Lady Judith," he said.

She nodded.

"I foolishly thought I cared for her, but as soon as my uncle died and my cousin went from heir apparent to earl, she announced her engagement to him." He scoffed. "Which meant I was heir presumptive. Every woman in England suddenly no longer cared if I spoke with a Scottish brogue and flocked to me like I was the most fascinating bit of man they'd ever seen." He frowned at the memory. "I wanted to be done with England, with the whole lot of it."

"James, I'm so sorry." She put her hand on his chest as though she could absorb the hurt from his heart with it.

"I'm no'," he replied. "My life would have been far worse if I'd married Lady Judith. Ye saved me from that fate." He caressed Penelope's soft cheek.

"And how did you become a valet for Lord Benton?" She raised her brows.

He cast her a chagrined look. "Ye've heard, then."

"I did, but you needn't think I care."

"How about ye?" He brushed a stray lock behind her ear. "Ye were the most sought-after woman on the marriage mart from what I hear of it. Why dinna ye wed?"

"I'm sure you know," she replied.

"Society's restrictions on women," he surmised.

"I have no desire to be owned by any man."

"I'd no' ever want to own a woman." He ran a hand down her waist, his touch light over her smooth, fair skin. "I like what we have. We're equal."

"It seems this has worked out quite well for us both." She cast him a sensual look that made his cock stir.

Not again tonight. He'd never had a virgin before, but he knew there would no doubt need to be a time of healing.

"Indeed, it has and will continue to do so," he said. "Life has dealt me a fine hand of late. I've a bonny wife who listens to my prattle on history and a feisty grandmother to keep me in check. I imagine it will continue to get on well. At least once I figure out

94

the agricultural details behind a Norfolk four course system on my estates."

"Norfolk four course system?" She smiled. "Is that an eating schedule for livestock?"

"That's what I said." He traced her collar bone with the pad of his middle finger. "I can tell ye all about it if ye'd like me to help put ye to sleep."

"I think I'd like to hear it." She lowered her head and nestled against him.

She didn't move at all in the time he talked, going on about the land and how the fields were swapped regularly, reiterating everything he'd found on the subject. After a bit of time, her shoulders rose and fell with a slow rhythm and he knew she'd gone to sleep.

He stopped talking, but he did not fall asleep. Not when holding her to him appealed to a deeper part of him than he had anticipated. He'd had lovers in the past, of course, but none of them had ever had their curiosity piqued by his historical knowledge. Certainly, none had ever asked about his past, not with the soft, genuine interest Penelope had.

And even if they had, he realized, he would never have shared. What was it about Penelope that made her so comfortable to talk to?

Whatever it was didn't make him want her any less. In fact, he found that after having her, he simply wanted her more. And in a marriage where he was supposed to be guarding his heart, that was not a good sign.

❧ 10 ❧

MacKenzie woke to a naked woman standing beside the bed. Which was precisely how he wished to wake up every morning.

Penelope glanced in his direction. Her eyes went wide as a squeak issued forth from her lips and she dashed behind a screen with a bit of muslin trailing after her. "Forgive me," she called out. "I rise early. I was trying to be quiet."

"Ye dinna need to apologize." He forced himself from the bed and pulled on his pantaloons. "I certainly dinna have any complaints at such a sight first thing in the morning." He picked up his shirt and put his arms through the sleeves before gathering up the remainder of his clothing. "I'll leave ye to dress."

He opened the door and hastened to his own chamber to give her privacy. He arrived at breakfast an hour later, but Penelope was not there. Gemma was, however, and engaged him in a dissertation of who wore what and which dance people danced with whom. In truth, MacKenzie only recognized a handful of the names she mentioned, but he nodded with interest regardless.

Gemma glanced toward the door; her face benign. "I don't suppose Lady Oakhurst will be joining us for breakfast?"

Penelope's toast points sat cold on a plate at MacKenzie's right. "I think ye're right." Disappointment squeezed at him before he shoved the useless emotion aside.

"Oh. I see." Gemma casually lifted the silver tongs and dropped another lump of sugar into her tea. A maid entered and she offered the young woman a broad smile. "I'll have a pastry please, one with a bit of strawberry jam in the middle."

The maid nodded and made to quit the room when Gemma called her back once more. "And one with a bit of marmalade as well."

The maid nodded once more and was gone.

MacKenzie regarded his grandmother, who had always possessed an affinity for sweets. "Ye know that just because she's no' here to see ye doesna mean yer toe doesna know ye're eating it."

"I'll be more mindful when I'm a great-grandmother." Gemma delivered a pointed stare and waved her fingers at him. "Off with you. I'm sure you have correspondence to tend to."

MacKenzie got to his feet and Gemma turned the side of her face in his direction. He chuckled and kissed her cheek before going about his business. After several hours in his study poring over an endless series of accounts, he had need for a text on agriculture from the library.

Requiring a stretch and a break, coupled with his natural inclination to not rely on the servants, he made his way to the library where he discovered the door slightly ajar. A curious thing indeed when he knew their housekeeper to be a stickler about checking small things, like doors being completely closed.

He pushed into the room and found Penelope standing before the section of medical texts. A swift peek around her revealed a book bound in crimson leather in her hands. A smile tugged at his lips. He only knew of one book with a crimson leather cover. It was one that had arrived with all of her other texts and contained many lurid images of couples in various forms of copulation.

97

It made for an interesting read; he would give her that.

He pushed the heavy oak door shut. The click was like a gunshot in the quiet room. She leapt at the sound and the book fell from her hands, where it slapped hard against the wooden floor.

She spun about, her cheeks flaming with guilt.

"I dinna mean to startle ye," he said, only partially lying. "What were ye reading?"

"Hmmm?" She raised her brows. If he hadn't seen the book himself, he'd think she was entirely innocent.

He held back his grin. "The book ye were reading when I walked in."

Her hand fumbled behind her to the shelf where she plucked a random text and held up the plain brown cover. "This? Oh, it's just..." She flicked her gaze to the text, and he swore he almost saw her grimace. "A book on farming."

"What was yer favorite chapter?" he asked.

"The first one," she replied simply. "It was all I managed before you entered the room and surprised me."

He hummed in understanding as he approached and bent to retrieve the crimson-bound book behind her. "I personally found page eighty-five particularly interesting."

She flushed but didn't lower her gaze. "Truly? The one on ninety-eight was far more fascinating."

He flipped through the pages to page ninety-eight where a man was drawn with his head between the woman's legs. "Indeed."

"I believe your book was placed accidentally with my medical texts." There was no accusation in her tone, but a hint of coyness that made MacKenzie's cock stir.

Still, the idea was so unexpected that a laugh burst from him. "I wouldna do such a thing."

Her brow furrowed. "Then how did it become mixed with my library?" She paused and grimaced. "The book...the inappropriate gown..." She put her hand to her brow and groaned. "My mother."

MacKenzie tilted his head. "Yer mother?"

"Has the post been delivered?" Penelope asked abruptly.

MacKenzie blinked at the sudden change in conversation. "I believe so. I received correspondence from my steward just this morning."

"And nothing else has arrived?" She slid the crimson book back onto the shelf.

MacKenzie shook his head. "I can summon George if ye like."

"It isn't George I believe to be at fault." She offered a faltering smile and shifted her attention across the room. But not before he caught the flash of disappointment.

"Ye've no' heard back from St. Thomas's I presume," he surmised.

Penelope swallowed. "Correct. Or rather from Dr. Cooper, as he is the one who revoked my ability to attend the hospital as an unmarried woman."

"I see." MacKenzie checked his watch. The hour read just past two, which meant he'd have enough time to pay a call before parliament began.

"I'm sure ye'll hear from him soon." He reached out a hand before he could stop himself and trailed his finger down her soft cheek and toward her lovely mouth. "In the meantime, I'll tell George to be vigilant for the arrival of any missives and come to ye immediately upon receiving one."

He let his hand fall away and Penelope pressed her lips together slowly, as though savoring the caress. "Thank you, James."

He pulled the crimson book off the shelf once more and handed it to her with a wink. "I shall leave ye to yer reading, my lady." With that, he strode from the room and informed George to not only watch for incoming mail, but also to ready the carriage.

Unbeknownst to Dr. Cooper, MacKenzie would be having an impromptu meeting with the President of the Chirurgical Society of London. No matter what it took, MacKenzie would ensure by the end of the meeting, Penelope was accepted back at St. Thomas's. He was a gentleman, yes, but he could be base when it served him best.

After all, he was not a Wicked Earl for nothing.

THREE DAYS LATER, PENELOPE WAS BACK AT ST. THOMAS'S Hospital, much to the displeasure of Dr. Bailey. She'd received the letter from Dr. Cooper welcoming her back just that morning and was able to resume her usual tasks of assisting surgeons with their work, as well as taking on some minor cases on her own.

Returning to the bustle of the hospital was like breathing again. It pacified a need inside of her nothing else could touch. It was knowledge and curiosity bundled together in an exhilarating package whose contents were always new and surprising.

She relished everything from bundling the lengths of linen to be used for bindings to the energized rush of an emergency. Before she realized it, the day had slipped by without her knowing. Already, the sun had set and there was no doubt she would be late for dinner.

She knew James and his grandmother would not be cross with her, but still it displeased her that she'd been so careless of the time.

The thought of James made her cheeks go hot. As it always did.

They often spent apart their days, only crossing from time to time in the library. Their nights, however, were enjoyed together as they explored every part of one another in intimate, lurid detail until both were slick with sweat and exhausted from spent pleasure.

James had been correct. Page eighty-five was indeed interesting. Though thirty-two and seventy-eight held their own appeal as well.

Quickly, Penelope performed one final round on the patients who had been in her care that day and still remained. One bed, however, she found empty.

A dresser stood near it. The dresser assisted the physicians and surgeons with bandaging wounds of patients, taking their notes and doing minor tasks such as stripping the mattress of its linens, as he did now.

"What happened to this patient?" she asked. "He'd come in with a gangrenous toe. Surely, he was not sent on his way after its removal."

The dresser shrugged. "He died, as far as I understand it. Dr. Bailey took his toe and the man did not survive the procedure."

Penelope hid her surprise that Dr. Bailey had performed the surgery when he of all people would see a surgeon's job as beneath him.

"I see," Penelope said slowly. "Thank you."

Death was not uncommon in St. Thomas's. Hospitals were not safe places for people who were unwell with so much illness about, but it was often the only option for many deficient in adequate income. No doubt the patient had other ailments that had prevented his body from rallying after the shock of a removed appendage.

And yet, the young man had seemed so healthy when he'd arrived.

Penelope left the room and caught sight of a petite brunette with a square set to her shoulders heading in her direction.

"Miss Elizabeth," Penelope said with a smile.

The older nurse stopped in her tracks and offered an exaggerated curtsey. "Lady Oakhurst." She offered Penelope a rare grin. The woman had elbowed her way into a world of men with an aggressiveness Penelope could appreciate. Miss Elizabeth was a force to be contended with when one opposed her, and a fierce and loyal companion should one be so lucky as to call her a friend.

And Penelope was lucky indeed to have a woman such as her as an ally.

"Oh, you needn't bother with all that." Penelope waved her hand.

"Welcome back, my lady." The nurse waggled her brows. "I heard your husband went to Dr. Cooper on your behalf. Threatened to punch him no less, if you were not reinstated."

"Did he?" Penelope asked, horrified.

Miss Elizabeth appeared nonplused. "The pompous ass probably deserved it." She chortled. "How were your patients today? Did they make you wish you were still far from the hospital?"

"Not at all. It's wonderful to be back. Only..." Penelope lowered her voice. "Did you see the patient this morning with the toe that required removal?"

Miss Elizabeth grimaced. "I certainly remember that toe."

"And what about the man himself?"

They both shifted out of the way as a surgeon strode by with a bloodied apron. "Fit as a fiddle," Miss Elizabeth said. "Easy on the eyes too."

Penelope leaned closer to ensure no one would hear her. "He didn't survive the surgery. Dr. Bailey apparently performed the procedure. I don't—"

"Don't go stirring up trouble just yet on your first day returned, my lady." Miss Elizabeth glanced about and whispered, "Dr. Bailey has started handling some of the surgeries of late. Several have not had good outcomes."

A cold knot of fear tightened in Penelope's stomach as she recalled having questioned Dr. Bailey prior to her prompt dismissal from the hospital.

"You'll wrinkle that pretty brow furrowing it so much." The nurse tilted her head toward the doorway. "Put it from your thoughts and get home in time for a proper dinner with your new husband, eh?"

"Of course," Penelope eased her face into the amiable mask she'd spent a lifetime wearing. But the concern about Dr. Bailey did not abate. At least not until she found herself downstairs and discovered it was not her mother waiting for her, but James.

Excitement fluttered low in her belly at the sight of him, regal and handsome with a silk cravat and a green waistcoat that turned the moss of his eyes to a deeper shade of green.

"Good evening, Lady Oakhurst." He gallantly offered her his arm. "I asked yer mother for the privilege of seeing ye home. She was quite excited at the prospect and agreed before I could even complete the request."

Penelope laughed as she slid her hand into the crook of his elbow. She hadn't noticed how chilled her fingers were until they met the heat of his body. He always ran hot, which she greatly appreciated because she always ran far too cold.

"I'm surprised she did not set you up to the task herself." Penelope looked up at him. He'd shaved recently, as not a whisper of a beard showed on his smooth jaw. For her? "Did your grandmother suggest you come?"

James led her out into frigid night air where their carriage awaited. "Well, yes."

A flash of disappointment struck Penelope, as swift as it was surprising.

"But no' before I'd made the decision to come myself." James winked at her and sent Penelope's heart pounding. "She did, however, suggest I inform Lady Bursbury of my intent to ensure she dinna take the time to do it herself, which I'd egregiously no' considered prior to her consideration."

Penelope climbed into the carriage and James followed, settling himself in the padded seat opposite her, his face suddenly serious. "I wanted to ensure they dinna give ye any difficulty on yer first day. Specifically, regarding Dr. Bailey."

His concern brought a grateful smile to her lips. "That was kind of you. Thank you."

The carriage rolled forward in the direction of Oakhurst Place. Home. It was a curious thing how quickly she'd come to think of it as such.

"I heard you visited Dr. Cooper on my behalf." Penelope studied James for his reaction.

He shrugged. "Some men need to be nudged toward the path of reason."

Penelope cleared her throat. "Did you also threaten to assault him?"

"Some men need a harder nudge than others." He leaned forward and took her icy hands in his larger, warm ones. "Ye're damn good at medicine, Penelope. Better than most of the butchers they employ at St. Thomas's or any other hospital in London. I've seen what ye've done for my grandmother and know what ye could do for others. Those men are fools for having forced ye out."

Penelope's heart caught in her chest. Aside from her mother, no one had ever stood so stoically at her side in support of her practice of medicine.

"Ye met their requirements to return," James continued. "There was no' a single reason why they shouldna have invited ye back the day after our wedding. Especially considering the heavy sacrifice on yer part by marrying me." He gave her a roguish grin.

"It hasn't been so terribly difficult," she confessed.

"That's verra kind of ye to say." He rubbed his thumb over the back of her hand. "Now tell me how everything went today."

Penelope regarded him, feeling a new sense of shyness with her husband she hadn't felt before. "I don't want to bore you."

"Ye never bore me. Quite the opposite, actually."

And with such a reply, how could she not comply with his request? She told him about her day and the patients she saw, and even about Dr. Bailey and her suspicions. The latter made his eyes narrow with a protectiveness Penelope found she rather liked.

That night when they were alone in her chamber, their bodies naked and entwined, she found herself unable to take her gaze from her husband and unable to stop the swelling of her heart within her chest. Of course, it didn't actually swell. She knew the science behind the organ's shape and its inability to increase in a healthy chest.

However, she also knew what was happening to her was not at all physical, but entirely emotional. And that was what scared her most.

For all of the schemes her mother had employed, Penelope now feared it was not James who had been susceptible, but Penelope herself who had gone and fallen in love.

❧ 11 ❧

J ames couldn't concentrate on anything in front of him. He pushed aside the account ledgers he'd been going over. And over. And over. All without actually seeing a line of it. Not when his thoughts were anchored on Penelope.

He didn't like her suspicions of Dr. Bailey. And he especially didn't like how the worry of it plucked at her. Penelope was not the kind of woman who would simply dismiss such a thing as a physician ill-handling his patients. She was too fervent in her drive to understand everything. Except what had made her so good at medical practice could now perpetuate a very serious, very real danger.

What troubled him even further was his concern of her. She was his wife, of course. That, and he'd always been raised to protect women. But there was something more...

How he felt about her.

The only time he'd ever had even a whisper of the emotion in his chest now was with Lady Judith. And that paled in comparison to the hum spreading through him when he thought of Penelope.

His mouth lifted in a smile as he recalled the night before, how she had practically glowed with excitement as she told him about her day at the hospital. And how she asked each night for him to tell her a story of ancient Greece, or any of the other historical tidbits he could impart upon her.

He also recalled how she had looked at him later that night when they were alone. As though she wanted to memorize every detail of him. And how he'd already memorized every detail of her.

"Are you free at the moment?" A voice broke through his musing.

James lifted his head to find Gemma standing in the doorway.

He grinned at her. "For ye, Gemma, always."

She strode into the study, absent the cane she no longer required, and lowered herself into the chair opposite him. "Lady Judith called on me earlier today."

"Thank ye for no' inviting me to join ye."

Gemma cast him a chastising look that he responded to with a shrug.

"She's quite upset about your marriage," Gemma continued. "She believes you wed simply to avoid her."

"She's no' wrong." James leaned back in his chair.

"She also believes your marriage to be a sham." Gemma sighed. "A marriage of convenience." She raised her brows in silent question, clearly seeking confirmation.

"It was a swift marriage, Gemma."

"That isn't an answer, James." Gemma lifted her chin. "Did you two form a pact to wed without love?"

James sat forward in his seat and put his elbows on the table. "We did."

Gemma nodded, as though her suspicions had been confirmed. "And you do not love her?"

"No." James answered the question readily, and yet the response did not feel right even as he said it.

"You are a liar, James MacKenzie." Gemma stood up and planted her palms on the surface of the desk.

He winced at her accusation. "I dinna mean any harm by our agreement to wed, Gemma. I couldna stomach the idea of a marriage to Lady Judith—"

"I don't mean that you lied about the marriage of convenience," Gemma said. "We all knew that. I mean that you are lying to yourself about not being in love with your wife."

"In love?" MacKenzie scoffed. "I'm no' one to fall in love."

"But you are." This time, Gemma spoke more gently. "At least you once fancied yourself in love with Lady Judith, before she chose Gilbert."

He glowered. "I thought I did at the time. If the man I am today could go and speak to the boy I was then..." He shook his head. "I dinna know love then and dinna understand what it was."

"And you know love now." Gemma's eyes gleamed with her victory. "James, you love the woman you married. I see it in the way you discuss your interests with her and how fascinated she is by you. I see it in the way the two of you act around each other with gentleness and respect and a shyness that is terribly endearing. I even see it now in how you say you didn't understand love with Lady Judith. Because you understand it now, don't you?"

MacKenzie shifted uncomfortably in his chair. "That isna the kind of marriage I have with Penelope."

Gemma stared down at him from beneath her frilly lace cap. "Do you know what I think?"

"Why do I fear ye'll tell me regardless of what I say?" MacKenzie muttered.

"Because you know me well, James." She smiled tenderly at him. "And I know you. Penelope has always been part of the ton. She's always been sought after. And she doesn't care a whit. Her lack of concern has finally made you understand the truth even I had not realized all this time. That acceptance by society does not make a man or a woman. It is their actions, their love."

To this, MacKenzie simply grunted.

She glanced up at the bracket clock on the wall. "Aren't you supposed to be on your way to St. Thomas's to see her home?" Her mouth curled up at the corners. "Tonight would be an excellent time to tell her how you feel." The advice was offered in a sing-song tone that reminded him a bit too much of Lady Bursbury.

MacKenzie pushed himself to his feet to leave. "Ye'll do anything for a great-grandchild, won't ye, Gemma?"

MacKenzie's grandmother folded her arms over her chest. "Don't put me to the test, my boy. Lest you find out I'm quite the one to contend with."

"And that's why I love ye." He pressed a kiss to her soft, powdered cheek and made his way down to the waiting carriage.

While he traveled the short ride to St. Thomas's, Gemma's words played in his head. He shifted on the padded cushion, crossing one ankle over the other knee and then switching to the other side. Restless.

Like his mind.

But not his heart.

Because though he wished he could discount everything Gemma had said, he could not. Not when she had spoken such truth. It was foolish and reckless and dangerous. But he could not help himself from finally acknowledging that he was in love with Penelope.

THERE HAD BEEN NO MORE NEFARIOUS ACTS AT THE HOSPITAL. At least none that Penelope had seen during her second day back at St. Thomas's. And she had been looking.

The patients came in with the usual maladies and were handled accordingly. A few men with cuts from street brawls that were sent to a dresser to bandage their wounds, several who were ill and assigned to beds for monitoring, and an aging man whose chest caused him massive pain. And between it all, Penelope had worked alongside Miss Elizabeth, wrapping strips of linen and re-organizing the vials of medicines that were forever being set hastily in a bin for return to the cabinet.

Penelope nearly asked Miss Elizabeth if she'd seen anything else suspect, but the other woman's wary eye stayed Penelope's tongue. No, if Penelope was going to find something, she would have to do it herself.

A bellow of pain came from the hall—a sound so intense, Penelope nearly dropped the glass bottle in her hands. Miss Elizabeth cast a bored look over her shoulder, but Penelope set the medicine aside and rushed from the room.

A man writhed on a stretcher as he was carried through the hospital. He hollered again and grabbed at his thigh; below the knee, his leg was little more than pulpy skin and fragments of bone.

"What's happened?" Penelope asked a short, slender surgeon named Mr. Garrison.

He pushed his spectacles up his nose. "He was working with two large slabs of marble and one fell on his leg. The piece was too heavy to get off him and he was desperate..." He shook his head.

Penelope inwardly flinched, unable to keep from imagining such a terrible thing.

"The leg will need to be removed then?" she asked quietly.

Mr. Garrison pressed his lips into a thin line and nodded.

Penelope fell back to allow Mr. Garrison to be on his way to see to removing the man's leg. Though she'd tried often to assist in amputations, it was one of the few tasks she had not been allowed to attend. Doubtless due to her "delicate feminine sensi-bilities" or some such nonsense.

She set it from her mind. After all, it was nearly time for her to go home and she refused to be late this time, especially after dinner had been held for her the day before. She went upstairs to see to the patients she had cared for earlier in the day. Once she completed her rounds, she bade Miss Elizabeth a good evening, then practically ran straight into someone as she rounded a corner too quickly.

"Forgive me." She backed up to put space between them and recognized the man as Mr. Garrison.

He smiled and his eyes crinkled with kindness. "Don't trouble yourself over it, Lady Oakhurst."

She tilted her head. "I thought you would be rather consumed with the man's leg."

Mr. Garrison shook his head. "Dr. Bailey is seeing to his surgery."

A chill descended on Penelope's heart. "Dr. Bailey?"

He nodded. "Have a pleasant evening, Lady Oakhurst." He inclined his head respectfully and went on his way down the hall, whistling a small tune to himself.

Penelope stood stock-still for a moment. She should not force her way into a room where an amputation was being performed. Really, she ought to head downstairs where James was already no doubt waiting for her.

But worry nipped at the back of her mind as she once more recalled the man with the gangrenous toe. He'd been too young, too healthy to die from the shock of losing so small an appendage. It was then she noted an eerie silence around her. The man with the leg had stopped crying out.

That final comprehension made up her mind for her. She turned in the opposite direction of the stairs that would lead toward the exit of St. Thomas's and instead made her way toward the rooms used for amputation.

The first few doors revealed empty rooms. The third, however, displayed the man with the mangled leg stretched out on a bed. A metal framed device lay over his face with a hose affixed to it.

"What is the meaning of this?" Dr. Bailey demanded angrily from the other side of the room.

"What is the meaning of *this*?" Penelope countered, indicating the patient. "Is this why your patients are dying after simple procedures?"

The man on the bed did move. She made her way closer.

"That's enough." Dr. Bailey strode toward her, his gait clipped. "Leave at once."

Penelope didn't leave. She wouldn't. Not this time. "Is he dead?" she demanded.

"He's been exposed to high levels of carbon dioxide and is in a state of sleep so deep that he will not feel the pain of his limb being removed."

"So deep that he may die," she surmised.

Dr. Bailey narrowed his eyes.

"Like the man yesterday with the gangrenous toe." She lifted her chin. "What you are doing lacks ethics and morality. You are sacrificing lives that need not be lost."

"I am advancing our knowledge of medicine," he hissed.

She shook her head. "You are killing healthy patients. I'm reporting you to Dr. Cooper. The Medical and Chirurgical Society will put an end to this madness." She went for the door with purpose.

And did not get very far.

Pain exploded at the side of her head and the world spun about for one dizzying moment before she found the ground rising up to meet her. She tried to scramble to her feet, but a strong arm grabbed her by the waist and tugged her backward.

Panic pierced through the haze of her mind.

Struggle.

Fight.

And fight she did. With arms and legs flailing, feet kicking. But the arm locked around her remained in place. Like iron.

"Calm yourself, Lady Oakhurst," Dr. Bailey said smoothly into her ear.

He readjusted his grip on her and she managed to get one arm free. She slammed her fist back with all the strength she had and experienced the satisfaction of it meeting something incredibly hard. Agony splintered through her fingers and Dr. Bailey grunted in apparent pain.

His hold on her tightened, squeezing. Hurting.

Her thoughts flitted about errantly despite the danger of the situation. It made concentrating difficult and left her with a heaviness to her limbs. She gritted her teeth.

It was a symptom of having been struck hard in the head. Logically, she knew that. She'd seen it before in patients. Now with such addled confusion, she understood what they endured.

Dr. Bailey pushed something toward her face. Penelope's heart ceased for one terrifying moment. The metal-framed mask. White, thick paper lined the inside of it. She jerked her head to the side in an effort to avoid it pressing against her.

The movement made the thoughts swim about in her mind, as though her brain were floating wildly about in her skull. It took only that one brief moment, that hesitation as she acknowledged the intense discomfort, for him to crush the mask against her face.

Air rushed toward her and suddenly she could not breathe. She gasped, panting, trying to draw in whatever she could. Her damaged mind ached in hollow throbs.

"Everyone knew you didn't want to get married," Dr. Bailey whispered in her ear. "And opium is so accessible in the hospital. Many people fall prey to it, especially when going through a difficult event in their life. It would be so easy to accidentally take too much to allay the stress of an unwanted husband."

Darkness dotted Penelope's vision. She tried to shake her head but did not have the strength for even that.

James.

She would never see him again, be held by him again. She would never be able to tell him she loved him. A soft whimper escaped from her throat and the room faded to black.

❧ 12 ❧

MacKenzie waited patiently for Penelope near the entrance of the hospital where the smells were less offensive. Penelope might be able to overlook the smells associated with her passion, but James was still keenly aware of the sickly-sweet odors of illness, exacerbated by windows shuttered against the cold. All of this was overlaid with the sharpness of vinegar.

A woman bustling by paused and regarded him. "Lord Oakhurst, I presume?" She assessed him with a frank stare.

"Ye presume correct." He inclined his head. "Are ye one of my wife's friends?"

"Yes, I'm Elizabeth." Her brow furrowed and created a map of wrinkles suggesting she was older than he had originally assumed. "She said she was leaving nearly half an hour ago."

A chill slid down MacKenzie's spine. "Perhaps she is with a patient?" he asked warily.

"They were all fine." Miss Elizabeth cast an anxious glance behind her. "She'd checked on them before leaving."

"I need ye to take me to her," MacKenzie demanded.

Miss Elizabeth hesitated.

"She told me she expressed her concerns about Dr. Bailey to

ye," he said in a fierce voice. "If she is missing, she may be in danger."

Miss Elizabeth hissed out a breath. "Very well. Come this way."

She led him up the stairs at a brisk pace that suggested his assumption was correct: she too found Penelope's delay distressing. Energy pumped through MacKenzie's veins as he followed Miss Elizabeth deeper into the hospital.

"Where is Dr. Bailey?" she demanded of a man she passed.

The man cast him an odd glance in MacKenzie's direction and pointed down the hall. "He's in surgery——"

If he said anything else, neither MacKenzie nor Miss Elizabeth heard him as they raced in the direction he'd indicated. She pushed open the first door and revealed an empty room. MacKenzie pushed open the second. Nothing.

He clenched his fist. He hoped to God he was wrong. That Penelope would walk in and laugh at him for his worry.

Except the twist in his gut told him his concern was not unfounded.

Miss Elizabeth shoved at the third door and cried out. MacKenzie raced into the room and found exactly what Miss Elizabeth had.

Penelope lay on the hard floor in a rumpled state, her face pale, her eyes closed, while a tall, slender man leaned over her with a cup at her lips. He started at the intrusion and his stricken expression told MacKenzie everything he needed to know.

The physician was not helping Penelope. He was hurting her.

MacKenzie didn't pause. He didn't think. His rage took control of him and sent him sailing through the air at the man who meant Penelope harm.

MacKenzie's body collided with the physician, sending the smaller man flying off her.

"Ye bastard," MacKenzie growled. "Why dinna ye fight someone who can defend themselves, aye?" He drew back a fist and slammed it twice into the man's face: once for Penelope and a second time to knock him unconscious.

The physician's body went slack. MacKenzie didn't even wait to see him fall before turning to his wife.

Miss Elizabeth sat by her side, holding Penelope's limp wrist between her hands.

MacKenzie's heart stopped. Penelope was too still. Her face too drained of color.

"Is she...?"

"She's alive," Miss Elizabeth said. "But her pulse is weak." She lifted the cup Dr. Bailey had dropped on the floor and sniffed. "Laudanum. A fair amount by my estimation. Enough to kill her."

MacKenzie tensed.

"There's a considerable amount on the ground." Miss Elizabeth pushed to her feet. "I'll send for a physician to tend to Lady Oakhurst, summon the Runners for Dr. Bailey and get a surgeon to see to this poor blighter here." She nodded to the man on the table in the center of the room. A white sheet lay over the man up to his chest, the bottom of which MacKenzie could now see was stained crimson with blood.

Good God. What the devil had the physician been doing?

"Don't move her," Miss Elizabeth cautioned as she quit the room.

MacKenzie sank to his knees at Penelope's side and called her name softly, but she didn't respond. He lifted her hand, tucking it gently within his own. Her fingers were cold. As they always were.

Except instead of the endearing thought tugging a smile to his lips as endearing thoughts of Penelope often did, this one caused a knot of emotion in the back of his throat.

He wanted her at the hospital every day so he could listen to each of her new adventures and what she had learned. He wanted her nights and her days and the quiet breakfasts they shared.

He smoothed a lock of hair from Penelope's brow. His fingers came away smeared with blood. A second glance confirmed she was bleeding from near her temple.

His heartbeat came faster. Harder.

Had Miss Elizabeth seen the blood? Had she known Penelope had been struck? Did that change anything?

MacKenzie might not have a curiosity for medicinal knowledge like Penelope, but he knew a good knock to the head could kill a man. Or a woman.

He shook his head and drew in a shaky breath. "Penelope, please."

She didn't respond. Penelope. His wife. The one he was certain he wouldn't love. And he'd squandered the time they had spent together with lies to himself.

"I love ye," he whispered in a choked voice. "Please, Penelope...please wake up."

Heat prickled at his eyes and nose, but he didn't care. Not even when several men rushed into the room with Miss Elizabeth behind them. Two lifted the stretcher of the man under the bloody sheet. Two more who were thick with muscle went to Dr. Bailey whose groans indicated he was waking, and one knelt at Penelope's other side.

"She's bleeding." MacKenzie indicated the blood at the side of her head. "She was struck." His voice was thick with emotion.

The surgeon at Penelope's side hummed in a sound of acknowledgement and put a small horn to her chest. The man placed the attached tubes into his ears, nodded and lifted each of her eyelids in turn, examining her eyes.

Miss Elizabeth went to the side of the bed where Dr. Bailey's contraption of a barrel, jars and tubes was still assembled. "What the devil is this?"

The surgeon looked up from Penelope. "I'll examine it in a moment." He turned his attention to MacKenzie. "Take her home. She's more at risk here than in her own bed due to contagion. Summon a private physician at once to see if there is more that he can do for her than I can."

MacKenzie gathered Penelope into his arms, desperate to get her from St. Thomas's hospital, away from the odors of illness and vinegar. He wanted her to have a proper physician, anyone that might give him some bloody answers and make sure Penelope would be safe.

She was slack in his arms. Like a doll. Unresponsive. She didn't move when he took her to the carriage, or when she was later placed into her bed.

MacKenzie had once thought the stretch of hours between their second kiss and the ball ending the night that they'd consummated their marriage had been interminable. And yet that time was nothing compared to the wait for the physician to finally arrive.

☙❧

PENELOPE'S HEAD ACHED. NOT IN ONE SPECIFIC SPOT, BUT throughout, as though her mind had been stuffed full of cotton. She concentrated through the pain to seek the primary spot of discomfort, to identify what she could do to alleviate the hollow, throbbing sensation.

Yes. There. At her temple.

She slowly opened her eyes as she reached for the spot.

"Dinna touch it." The familiar voice was filled with affection.

She slid her gaze to the side of the bed and there he was. James MacKenzie, the handsomest peer in all of London, possessing the most roguish smile. But he wasn't smiling now. He was leaning toward her with his brow furrowed in seriousness. He hadn't shaved in a while and a hint of a beard shadowed his hard jaw.

"What is it?" Penelope asked.

He frowned. "Do ye no' remember?"

MADELINE MARTIN

She frowned as well. Did she remember what? She took in her surroundings, recognizing at once that she was in her own chamber, the sheets of her bed soft and luxurious beneath her. But what had happened before?

A name rose in her mind, followed by the chill of recollection.

"Dr. Bailey," she said through numb lips.

James nodded and reached for her hand.

She let him enfold her fingers against the heat of his large palm. "Oh, James," she whispered. "He has been experimenting on patients. It's why he wanted me gone from the hospital. I had walked in on him that day and had no idea."

"He attacked ye," James said, his tone hard. "He hit ye on the head, then poisoned ye with carbon dioxide, then tried to kill ye with an excess of laudanum."

Penelope tensed, suddenly recalling everything. The need to breathe, the fear of death looming over her. The fear she might never see James again.

His eyes watered and the muscles of his jaw clenched. "I thought ye were dead, Penelope."

She tightened her grip on his hand. In truth, she had thought she would die too. Before she could tell him—

"I love ye, Penelope." His voice caught and her heart soared.

He lowered his head, as though he couldn't bear to meet her gaze. "I dinna want a marriage with love before, I know. It wasn't planned. I dinna count on how I would feel about ye. I know that this deviates from our original agreement, but—"

"James—"

"Ye dinna need to say anything," he rushed. "I dinna expect anything in return."

"I love you."

"When I almost lost ye..." His head snapped up and he met her gaze with one of bewilderment. "What did ye say?"

Penelope touched his face with her free hand and the whiskers along his jaw prickled against her palm. Everything

120

inside of her was warm and happy, as though all of her were internally glowing.

"I said, 'I love you.'" Her voice caught with emotion. "I never thought I could love someone other than my family, as though my heart was in some way broken, only functioning with purpose. I'm certain that sounds strange, but I never realized I could feel such emotion for someone else." She swept her thumb over his jaw. "Until you."

"That doesna sound strange to me." He released her hand and held her face. "When I was a lad, I remember my da telling me about Helen of Troy."

Penelope felt herself smile in anticipation for another bit of information about Greece's rich history. "Helen of Troy?"

He studied her as he spoke. "The face that launched a thousand ships and set the Trojan War into motion. I have often wondered how a woman's beauty, how the depth of care for her, could cause men to go to such lengths." His lips brushed hers. "I know now."

Penelope smiled at the most beautiful compliment she had ever received.

"So, ye see, my claim to love is just as strange, if not more so." James winked at her.

She nestled closer to him. "I love your knowledge of history and how you don't mind me prattling on about my studies. I love how there's a cultured air to you, as well as a dangerous one."

He grinned like a rogue and she completely melted.

"I love ye, Penelope MacKenzie. A woman whose beauty is only surpassed by her intelligence."

"You do know how to compliment a woman." She smiled up at her husband.

"Only the deserving ones."

Penelope lifted a brow.

"Meaning, ye and Gemma." His confession was so sheepish, Penelope couldn't help but give a small laugh. She winced slightly at the pounding in her head, exacerbated by conversation and her laughter.

James stroked the uninjured side of her head with soothing fingers. Penelope closed her eyes to the sensation. "That feels heavenly."

"Lie back and let me do it until ye fall asleep." His tone was velvety with temptation.

"I don't want to go to sleep," Penelope said. It was her turn to look sheepishly up at him. "I don't want you to go."

He settled into the bed beside her. "Then I'll stay right here at yer side."

Penelope snuggled closer to him as his fingers continued to play gently through her hair. The caress was calming. And she was so very tired still, her mind thick with the persistent ache of everything she had endured from Dr. Bailey's attack.

And as she started to fall asleep, James spoke once more, "I'll be here always, my love."

❧ 13 ❧

Penelope had celebrated Christmases through her life, of course, but never had a feast been thrown with such extravagance as the one James and his grandmother had orchestrated.

It had been done to get Penelope's mind off Dr. Bailey's trial. She knew this and appreciated it greatly. The doctor had been denounced in the medical texts circulating London, not only for the dozens of deaths he had been responsible for with his testing, but also his attack on Penelope.

And what a distraction the feast was. There was roast goose and mincemeat pies and several types of puddings. More food than any of them could possibly eat. Garlands of holly and evergreens covered every banister, accompanied by gold paper stars, while ivy hung like veils of lace over each doorway.

There was even a large evergreen tree set at the far end of the drawing room with small candles lit throughout its boughs.

"Aren't you afraid it will set the house afire?" Penelope's mother asked.

Penelope slid a glance toward James. Those had been her very words when he suggested it. "I've been reassured it will be fine."

"Aye." He put an arm around her shoulder. "They've been lighting candles in trees since Queen Elizabeth's reign."

Immediately, the heat of his strong body made her melt in the most wonderful way. Penelope edged closer to her husband, grateful for the feel of him against her.

"Did all the fires spreading through England make them stop?" Penelope's Uncle Noah asked.

Aunt Helen nudged his side and he spared her an affronted look.

"We can thank Oliver Cromwell for abolishing those Christmas festivities," James replied. "As well as many other nefarious deeds I'll no' get into on such a fine day of celebrating."

"I think it's all beautiful," Eugenia said, her eyes bright. "I want to have one in my house every year after I am wed."

"Have you a gentleman in mind already?" Penelope asked.

"No, but I'm sure Mama will find a suitable man to match me with." Eugenia glanced at Lady Bursbury with clear expectation.

"God help you," Noah muttered.

"I heard that, Noah." Lady Bursbury slid her brother a hard look, to which he simply replied with a smirk.

"Or maybe I'll introduce you as I did with Lord Oakhurst and our Penelope." Lord Bursbury adjusted his cravat. "Perhaps your mother isn't the only matchmaker in the family." He raised his brows playfully at Penelope's mother.

Lady Bursbury's mouth fell open. "Elias, don't you dare go on taking credit for this match. You know well and good they never would have fallen in love if it weren't for me."

"They'd never have had the chance, were I not there to introduce them." Lord Bursbury winked at Penelope, his eyes twinkling as he clearly had his fun with Lady Bursbury.

"Were it not for my gifts—"

"Gifts?" Eugenia piped in. "What gifts?"

"I believe this is the part of the conversation where we slide away," Penelope whispered to James. "I certainly don't want to hear the answer."

James looked toward Lady Bursbury's stricken face. "Oh, but I do."

The room fell silent as all eyes fell on Lady Bursbury, who stammered and stuttered before finally exclaiming, "Oh do look at the time! I feel we've stayed longer than is polite." She primly fluffed the flounces on her sleeves.

"Ah, that old trick." The tender smile on Uncle Noah's lips as he spoke said everything his jests did not.

Lady Bursbury swatted at him. "We must give Lord and Lady Oakhurst time to properly ready themselves to leave for Paris."

"That's not for several more days," Penelope said with a laugh.

"Well," Lady Bursbury sniffed. "You need to ensure you have everything you need, is what I meant."

"That's verra considerate of ye, Lady Bursbury." James inclined his head.

The carriages were summoned for Penelope's aunt and uncle as well as her parents, and farewells followed swiftly afterward.

Lady Bursbury was the last to leave as she fiddled with a bit of garland at the foot of the stairs.

"You were the one who suggested we take our leave, dearest," Penelope's father gently called in her direction. "Come on then, lest I match Eugenia before you get a chance, woman."

Lady Bursbury startled. "Oh, you wicked man, do not even set your mind to it." She rushed over, embracing first James's grandmother, then James. And then, finally, she came to Penelope, her face beaming.

Lady Bursbury settled her hands on Penelope's shoulders. "I'm so proud of you, daughter. I always have been."

Penelope smiled at her mother. "I know," she said honestly. "You've never made me feel ashamed of who I was, and you always encouraged me regardless. I'm so humbly grateful."

Lady Bursbury put a hand to her chest and her eyes misted

with tears. "No, don't. I can't go to the carriage in tears or I'll never hear the end of it from your father." She waved her gloved hand in front of her face as though that might dry her tears.

"Is there anything I ought to expect in my traveling trunks?" Penelope asked as she embraced her mother.

Lady Bursbury gently squeezed her daughter the way she always did when she hugged those she loved. "I make no promises," she said cheerily and was gone before Penelope could even open her mouth to comment.

"What are these?" Gemma asked from where she studied the garland at the foot of the stairs. "Weren't these at your wedding as well?"

Penelope approached with James following closely behind her. There, nestled among the gold paper stars was what appeared to be a gold paper liver, as well as gold paper lungs and a gold paper brain.

"Organs," Penelope said with a smile. "Several years back, we were asked to cut out stars for Christmas decorations. I had recently finished a fascinating account of the body's organs and did those instead of stars since I assumed they were simply for entertainment."

She gently brushed her finger over a delicate tissue-paper heart. "When I realized they were for decoration in the house, I immediately made stars instead. My mother said nothing and still hung the little organs up with all of the stars."

"She did it up the whole flight of stairs." Gemma looked up the banister then strode over to the bunch of holly running along the edge of a table.

Her gait was even and smooth, without a hint of the former hobble she'd exhibited when Penelope first met her. While the Dowager Lady Oakhurst indulged on occasion, it was rarely done, and her walks had been frequent, most of them with Penelope. It had strengthened the bond between them and helped Gemma's body fight off the effects of gout. And even if another flare up did occur, Penelope would be there to aid her.

"They're on this bunch of holly as well." Gemma pointed to the back table. "And there too. I see them."

Penelope grinned at the discovery. "My mother can work the most wondrous things when no one is looking."

"I'll no' disagree with ye on that." James slid his arm around Penelope's waist.

Her cheeks immediately heated, as well as other various locations. She looked up into his handsome face, and all of her felt as though it were smiling. He had shown her acceptance though she had never sought it from society, and he had helped her realize her heart could embrace someone beyond her family. That love and intellect could not only exist together but thrive in the most beautiful fashion.

"What are ye thinking when ye look at me like that?" he asked with that roguish grin of his.

"That I love you," she said with all the emotion in her soul.

He kissed her gently.

"This old woman knows when it's time to retire." Gemma rushed past them and made way for the stairs.

"Ye dinna need to, Gemma," James called after her.

"Bah!" She spun about and shook her finger at James. "I want a great-grandchild." Then she sweetly wished them a "Happy Christmas" and slipped up the stairs.

"I suppose we have our orders." James offered Penelope his arm and led her up the stairs.

"And what do you think of her demand?" Penelope asked, her pulse pattering a little faster. It was something she'd considered through the days following her realization that she truly did love James MacKenzie. "Even if it is outside of our initial negotiations."

James opened the door to their shared bedchamber; the large one he'd once occupied alone. He closed the door behind them and indicated the large bunch of mistletoe hanging along the doorframe above them.

He pulled her into his arms. "I think ye owe me a kiss."

⚜

JAMES WOULD NEVER BE UNAFFECTED BY HIS WIFE'S KISSES. HER lips were too soft, her sweet rose scent too alluring. And those sensual sounds she hummed in the back of her throat... Good God.

And yet, they had an important conversation to finish.

James nestled his face along the silky column of Penelope's throat. "Are ye wanting to stray outside of our original marital negotiations?" he asked.

She was silent a long moment.

He straightened and regarded her. A flush had blossomed over her cheeks and lips.

She nodded. "On two points specifically."

"Two?" He scoffed playfully.

"First," she continued. "I've decided I do not like the idea of you ever taking a lover and so I wish you to strike that from the list."

James couldn't help but grin at the note of contention. There was no other woman he wanted to be with other than Penelope. "Only if ye remove it from yers."

"Done." She lifted her chin. "And second, yes, I would like a child with you. One who has your dark hair and lovely green eyes."

"Lovely?" He tried to give her his most ferocious stare.

She laughed. "Lovely and quite masculine, I assure you."

He caught her hand and drew her closer to him as he considered her. It was almost too easy to imagine her round-bellied with his child and then later, holding a small babe with a fuzz of red hair atop its sweet head. His mouth lifted with a smile.

"I'd love to see ye as a mother," he replied in earnest. "And Gemma can occupy the children, along with their nanny, while ye're at the hospital."

"Children?" She ran her hand over his chest. "Already planning more than one?"

His body immediately responded to her touch, sending tingles of pleasure rushing through his blood. Especially to certain parts of him. "When should we start?"

"I've assessed myself and have determined I am entirely healthy and ready to get with child," she said confidently.

He raised his brows. "Have ye now?"

"Yes." She gave him a cocky smile that made him go hard as a rock. He loved her confidence when she spoke of her medical knowledge, how it squared her shoulders and set that glint in her eye.

"I can tell you with the certainty of a physician there are no lasting effects of carbon dioxide in my body," she continued. "Nor are there any remnants of the high dose of laudanum."

Thoughts of that attack on her only made him pull her tighter to him, as if he could always keep her so close to ensure she was protected.

"So, ye're saying we should start trying for a child now?" James trailed his fingertips down her collarbone.

Penelope breath hitched. "I imagine the time is optimal for...oh."

His touch had dipped inside the neckline of her dress, teasing at her nipple as it grew taut.

"I shall have to make sure I'm incredibly thorough." He reached around and unfastened the first two buttons of her gown.

She whimpered hungrily in response.

"I love ye verra, verra much, Penelope." He plucked free several more buttons.

And he *did* love her, for her intelligence, for her beauty, for the kindness of her generous heart, and for the acceptance she offered him that he'd always sought. She had made England his home.

He finished the row of buttons and slid the white gown from her body. Except it was not a basic chemise she wore beneath her clothing. It was the lacy one.

Good God.

It fit her body like a sensual glove, pink where her nipples strained against the delicate lace, and a shadow of auburn downy hair visible at the apex of her thighs.

MacKenzie's mouth went dry.

She smiled wickedly, the minx, and drew him toward their bed.

How he adored his wife. But now was not a time for talking, and so he showed her with his body, with their shared pleasure, exactly how much he loved her.

And how much he really liked that wispy bit of a chemise.

EPILOGUE

June 1826
Oakhurst Manor

Penelope put her stethoscope to the little boy's thin chest and smiled at the clear whoosh of air in and out of his lungs.

"Can you breathe for me, Timothy?" she asked. "Big and deep, like this." She huffed for him in exaggeration.

He laughed and did exactly as Penelope had instructed with all the gusto of a small boy trying to be bigger than he was. No coughing followed. A wonderful sign. Penelope concentrated on the air moving easily through his chest and stood up with authority.

"You sound like you have the healthiest set of lungs I believe I've ever heard." She put her hands on her hips. "You must have been taking all of your medicine."

He nodded vigorously.

"He has." His mother ruffled the boy's blond hair. "Can he run about with the others now? I've been holding him back for fear of making his breathing worse."

"There is no reason why he can't. He's quite recovered. In fact, with lungs such as his, I'm sure he'll best them all." Penelope winked at the little boy, who was already making his way for the door.

"Thank you, Dr. MacKenzie," the woman said in a rush as she ran off after her son.

Penelope watched the pair go, mother chasing after her healthy son, and contentment blossomed in her chest.

She was no physician. Such rights were still barred from women. But even though she'd told their tenants such countless times, they all insisted on calling her by the title, declaring she deserved it more than any physician they knew.

What was more, she did not charge the exorbitant fees of other physicians and treated anyone who came to her for free. Medical care should not be only for those whose pockets ran deep, but for those who were in need.

James had agreed with her logic and surprised her the first summer at Oakhurst Manor with a white building on their estate, stocked with a variety of necessary medical supplies. Her private hospital had been open since. A local midwife she'd been instructing operated it in her stead when she returned to London with James when he attended Parliament.

He'd made his own positive influence on the people of England with the acts he'd helped pass with his votes. There was an act to keep child workers from being exploited by cotton factories and another to protect cattle to ensure proper treatment of livestock.

Those months in the country, however, were always the happiest. Not just for her, but for James and their son, Arcas.

Movement caught her eye outside the window. She peered closer as several figures made their way to her hospital. Not new patients, but her family. James with Gemma on his arm and Lady

Bursbury beside them, with little Arcas leading the procession with great galloping leaps, his auburn hair rustling in the late afternoon light.

She went to the door and shielded the setting sun from her eyes. "Is it already time for supper?"

"Yes," Arcas shouted into the hot summer air. "And we're having trifle for dessert."

All at once, his giant leap into the air came down too hard and he tumbled forward. Both grandmothers exclaimed with more horror and emotion than they had ever done for their own children. As was the way when it came to grandmothers. Or so Penelope was learning.

For her part, Penelope went to her child and lifted him into her arms, though he was far too old to do so at five.

His chin quivered, but he bravely held his tears at bay. "My knee."

Penelope pushed aside the stubborn curl of hair at his forehead, just like his father's, and kissed his sweaty brow. "Let us get you into the hospital and I'll have a look at you."

"I'll play the part of stretcher." James swooped to her side and lifted Arcas from her.

She entered the building as James was settling Arcas onto the table and knelt by her son. That summer was the driest that had ever been seen in England. It made for a hard landing on a boy's skinny leg and blood smeared over the fresh scrape.

"Bend it for me," Penelope said.

He obediently bent his knee.

"Touch yer tongue to yer nose," James instructed.

Arcas laughed and stretched his tongue upward.

Penelope shook her head jovially at their antics. "Wiggle your toes."

Arcas wiggled his toes, but it was his father he looked up at with an expectant smile.

James arched a brow in challenge. "Wiggle yer ears."

Arcas scrunched his face in concentration, but his ears did not move.

Penelope got to her feet to fetch vinegar and plaster. "Your knee will be fine once I clean it."

"Aye, but yer ears might be broken," James added solemnly.

"James," Gemma chastised from the doorway.

He chuckled and wriggled Arcas's ears for him, then went out to occupy the grandmothers so Penelope could work in peace.

She took a bit of linen and a bottle of vinegar and sat in front of the table once more. "This may sting."

Her son watched her with wide green eyes and nodded with stoic resolve. "I can bear it."

"I know you can, my brave boy." Penelope wet the linen with a splash of vinegar.

"It's interesting—" Arcas hissed as the liquid stung at his cut. "The Greeks used vinegar to clean their wounds and we do the same."

Penelope focused on getting all the bits of grass and dirt from the wound, lest it become inflamed. Fevers were by far her biggest enemy and she'd not have one plague her boy. "That is interesting."

"One would think," he continued, "that in so many centuries of learning, we would devise a different method for cleaning a wound."

Finished, Penelope straightened and smiled down at her precocious son. "And perhaps, you will be the one to come up with it."

Arcas nodded, his brow furrowed with consideration. The look was a direct mirror image of the one his father gave while reading a particularly interesting new history book.

Penelope set aside the bottle of vinegar, applied a sticking plaster to the wound and helped him from the table. "I'm finished. Now tell me about that trifle."

"It has biscuits in it and a custard—that's my favorite part."

He led her outside where James was waiting with Gemma and Penelope's mother.

The women rushed to Arcas as though he was a soldier returned from battle, and Penelope went to her husband.

"Thank ye for saving his life." James kissed her and put his arm around her. "Now we'll just need to keep an eye on those two to make sure they dinna fight over him."

Gemma took one of Arcas's hands and Lady Bursbury took the other. The three began the short walk to the manor house.

"I think they'll be well-behaved," Penelope said.

"For now," James muttered as they strode together behind the trio.

Their shoes whispered over the dry grass and a balmy breeze blew at their faces. "I love these summer days," Penelope confessed.

"As do I." James squeezed her closer. "And I love seeing ye so happy here."

"I'm always happy with you, James MacKenzie."

"And I'm the luckiest man alive because of it." He positioned himself to block the bright sun from her eyes.

"You're about to be all the luckier." Penelope glanced up at him.

"Page thirty-five?" He grinned.

Page thirty-five was their favorite.

She lifted her brows at him to let him know she was most certainly amenable to page thirty-five, but then took his hand and put it to her lower abdomen. "It's been over eight weeks."

James sucked in a breath. "Penelope."

God, how she loved her husband. How simply stating eight weeks was met with understanding rather than questioning.

A smile blossomed on his face. "If it's a girl..."

"Yes," Penelope replied, fully expecting the question. "She will be named Athena."

His smile widened. "I love ye more than life itself."

"And I you, Husband." She stopped and rose on her tiptoes to press a kiss to his mouth.

"Keep that up, and page seventy-six may come into play as well." His expression turned wicked.

Penelope shivered with delight. "Promise?"

"Always." He glanced ahead where the trio were swiftly leaving them behind. "Did ye tell yer mother and Gemma yet?"

Penelope lifted her brows in skepticism. "As if they would keep it a secret from you."

He held his arm out to her. "Are ye ready to make them even happier than they already are?"

Penelope slipped her hand into the crook of his elbow, marveling as she always did how perfectly well that they fit together. "Most certainly."

Together they caught up with Arcas, Gemma and Lady Bursbury, and all sat down to a lovely dinner, a sweet dessert, and even sweeter news to follow.

For certainly, their life was one of great joy, filled with the richness of intelligent discussion, unconditional acceptance and, most importantly, that irrational, totally unexplainable emotion called love.

***

Thank you for reading EARL OF OAKHURST! Please know that I read all of my reviews and would love to know how you enjoyed the story, so please do leave a review.

I've written several books with matches Lady Bursbury has made - you can find them here:

Noah and Helen in MESMERIZING THE MARQUIS where a reclusive marquis finds a woman who just might soften his hard heart...

WWW.MADELINEMARTIN.COM/BOOK/MESMERIZING-THE-MARQUIS/

The Duke and Duchess of Stedton in DISCOVERING THE DUKE (Part of the DUKES BY THE DOZEN anthology) where the pair are reunited at a house party after a lackluster start to their marriage. Will a sizzling wager be enough to melt the frost between them, or will it truly remain the coldest winter in London?

www.madelinemartin.com/book/dukes-by-the-dozen/

And learn more about Alistair and Emma's story in EARL OF BENTON when a whisky smuggling earl does one last whisky run while trying to save an heiress whose uncle is determined to see her dead.

www.madelinemartin.com/book/the-earl-of-benton/

Make sure you join my newsletter to stay up to date on the latest Borderland Rebels news. Sign up today and get a FREE download THE HIGHLANDER'S CHALLENGE.
http://hyperurl.co/MMNL

READY FOR MORE WICKED EARLS? KEEP READING FOR AN exclusive excerpt from Aubrey Wynne's EARL OF DARBY:

Chapter One

Pendleton Place

Northern England
Early November 1819

HANNAH GLARED AT THE ARRAY OF CLOTHES SCATTERED ACROSS her rooms. Nothing seemed right, and she had to look perfect. Dresses and jackets spread across the counterpane, hanging from the bed posts, or draped over her dressing table. In the next room, petticoats, stays, and stockings were strewn over chairs and her traveling trunks. One table held shoes, slippers, and boots. There would be walks during the day, dances, and riding in Hyde Park. It would be her first extended visit away from home. She could be in London for up to six months, except the a trip home for Christmas and Twelfth Night celebrations, which her country neighbors still practiced with exuberance.

She fingered the pale pink muslin with tiny roses embroidered across the satin ribbon at the waist. The delicate flowers were repeated again across the hem and cuff. Would it make her appear too young? Would she look a total dolt against the backdrop of the elegant and polished beau monde?

Stop it! she scolded herself. Hannah was known for her poise and self-reliance. Why should her confidence falter over a trip to Town? Because Gideon would be there. Her stomach did a flip, her lips curving into an instantaneous smile. She closed her eyes, and his deep blue gaze, raven hair, and broad shoulders filled her vision.

Piffle! She needed to cease daydreaming about the earl. If only she could so easily quit a habit that had become second nature to her—since the day he'd stolen her five-year-old heart.

"A penny for your thoughts," whispered Eliza from behind.

She twirled around to find her sister-in-law with a hand over her mouth, surveying the windstorm that had come upon Hannah's rooms. "I'm selecting my clothes and having an odious time of it. I need to look sophisticated and show off my best features, yet young enough that I don't attract any vile old men."

"Of course, though I don't believe that's where your mind was just now," argued Eliza, rubbing her swelling belly. She looked lovely in the creamy morning dress, delicately embroidered at the cuffs and hem with a pale yellow that matched her flaxen waves. "What do you consider to be your greatest qualities?"

"That's the problem. They aren't visible. Intelligence, wit, common sense—"

"Humility..." Lady Pendleton's violet eyes shone with mischief.

"Merciful heavens, I don't think I've ever been accused of that, though I only believe myself to be passible pretty." She laughed and gave Eliza a hug. "How I will miss you, sweet sister."

"You'll be home before the new year. Perhaps even betrothed, for I don't think it will take long for someone to fall madly in love with you."

"But I only have eyes for one, and I hope this season will make him loony with jealousy and realize we are the perfect match." She sighed. "My first waltz shall be with Gideon. His strong hand on my waist, my palm against his. He will pull me close, our bodies in perfect harmony as he twirls me about the room."

"About Lord Stanfeld..." Eliza transferred a deep green riding habit from the bed to the post and sat. She patted a space next to her, waiting for Hannah to sit before she continued. "Nathaniel has returned with news."

Hannah's brother had gone to London on some business and to arrange for the townhouse to be opened. He most likely had seen his friends. "Is Gideon in good health? Has something happened to his mother, Lady Stanfeld?"

"Everyone is fine." Eliza paused. "Do you remember when he took his mother to Scotland?"

A knot began to form in Hannah's stomach. "Yes, his cousin was killed in that political demonstration, and the Stanfords went to offer their condolences." She didn't like the pitying expression in her sister-in-law' eyes. "He didn't marry?"

She shook her head. "No, but it seems he met someone, who Lady Stanfeld was also quite taken with, and she has returned with them."

A rock plummeted to the bottom of her belly, her chest tightening as she stared blindly at the Axminster carpet under her feet. He'd found another? She was just coming of age, and he couldn't wait a few more months? The selfish, thoughtless scoundrel. *Horse feathers!* Why she'd...win him over, of course. Hannah Pendleton was not one to give up easily.

"You say, he's not married?"

"No, but Nathaniel thought he sounded quite smitten." Eliza took Hannah's hand, sympathy darkening her eyes to a deep plum. "Stanfeld told your brother he plans on asking her as soon as the mourning period has passed."

"Mourning period? For a cousin?"

"The young lady is his cousin's widow."

Hannah let out a long whistle. "The proper Earl of Stanfeld wants to court the widow of his dead cousin?" She laughed then, relief untying the knot and disintegrating the rock in her stomach. "He must feel some kind of obligation toward her, and being from the Highlands, she is sure to have a certain charm. He will come to his senses."

She kissed her sister-in-law on the cheek and resumed her packing. Althea, Eliza's daughter from her first marriage burst into the room. "Oh, the pwetty clothes," exclaimed the toddler. "Are you putting them, Aunt Hannah? Can I watch?"

Hannah squatted down, her face level with the almost-four-year-old. "I'm so glad you've arrived. I want your opinion on each dress. Your mother and you will vote on which ones I shall pack and which shall stay behind. Can you help me?"

Althea clapped her hands, her blue violet eyes dancing with excitement, the black curls bobbing furiously as she nodded her head. "Oh, yes! Mama lets me pick out her dwesses when she's going some vewy important."

Hannah gave the little girl a hug. "I'll miss you so much, Thea."

"You will be back in two blinks, Mama said." Althea returned the hug and climbed onto the bed, leaning against her mother's swollen belly. "Nathaniel, it's me again, your big sistah." She kissed Eliza's stomach, then settled back against it.

With the help of her audience, Hannah finished packing. It took a bit longer than expected, with Althea piping in with opinions, trying a few articles on herself, and inviting her basset hound, Cyrano, to join the party. The dog didn't seem quite as happy as his mistress when a bonnet was wrapped around his head. When he began a long, soulful howl, Eliza packed up both dog and girl and bid Hannah good night.

Sleep did not come quickly with so many plans and thoughts of Gideon in her head. She dreamt of a prince, dark and handsome with smoldering dark blue eyes, and a princess with sepia hair and a gilded tiara sparkling with gems. They danced until she was breathless, and as he bent to kiss her, Hannah woke.

London
Mid-November 1819

THE TRIP WAS UNEVENTFUL, THE WEATHER PLEASANT, AND THE coach ride dull, dull, dull. Hannah had forgotten to pack her latest novel. Her brother, dear sweet Nathaniel, had unearthed an ancient magazine from an innkeeper's wife . She'd exhausted the pages of La Belle Assembleé. Thrice. She was now a fountain of knowledge concerning a wide variety of no-longer-pertinent subjects.

Masques, popular during the reign of James I, were at once a ball and an opera. *But a masquerade might be titillating,* she thought. *All those hidden faces identified only by the gleam in one's eyes or the devilish smile below the guise.* She'd found the Turkish tale of Jahia and Meimoune interesting the first read, the true story of George and Sophia better the second time, and never should have attempted the Fugitive Poetry section a third. The humorous anecdotes of famous French women had instigated a fierce bout of yawns. She knew what performances had been seen at Covent-Garden or the Cobourg Theater and what mourning fashion had been prevalent when Queen Charlotte died this time last year.

Hannah was not accustomed to being idle. She kept busy throughout the day, either practicing the pianoforte, embroidery, painting, walking, or riding her mare. Never sitting. Just sitting. Thank goodness there was a library at the townhouse. She would remember to bring several books for the journey home. She listened to her maid's soft snore and wished *she* could sleep in the dratted rocking vehicle. She should have brought her mare and been outside with her brother, but her mother had stomped her foot and forbade it.

The coach slowed as they finally encountered city traffic. The farther in to the town center, the more congested the streets. She flicked open the wooden slats and looked out at the clamor and overcrowded walkways. Parliament would assemble in another week or two, and the *ton* were gathering. The smells of the city assaulted her nose but she breathed in deeply, anticipating the coming adventure. The curses of coachmen, chatter of those on foot, and calls of vendors all combined into a background of chatter. The streets were still dry as the weather had been clear and no snow had fallen yet this season.

"How do you fare, sweet sister, with two days of inactivity?" Stanfeld's question floated through the narrow openings of the window. She could see strips of his dark great coat and black riding boots as he pulled up next to her. "One magazine and two days of nothing to do but look at your lady's maid."

"Which was why she chooses to ride in the rumble seat with the footman for the last leg of the journey. She'd rather face the chill than my sour countenance." Hannah chuckled. "Not that I blame her. I think that last accidental kick from my jiggling foot did her in."

"Aunt Bertie arrived ahead of us and, according to her note, has everything order." He winced. "I am sorry about being unable to stay and chaperone you myself. The timing couldn't be worse with Eliza."

"Don't be a ninny. I enjoy Aunt Bertie's outrageousness and am looking forward to it. Besides, I'd be disappointed in you if you weren't by Eliza's side. And Althea would be lost without at least one of us present."

"We'll have dinner with Stanfeld and Darby once we're settled in. They have been instructed to keep an eye on you and your chaperone. At least Darby's sister is also coming out, so you'll know someone before your first formal event."

"How old is Lady Matilda?" *Please don't let her be stunningly perfection.*

"Seventeen, I believe. Close to your age, of course." He grinned. "And she and Lady Darby will be a voice of reason, or a shield, when Aunt Bertie makes a sham of things."

"Perhaps our aunt has matured." Hannah rolled her eyes when her brother guffawed. "I mean, in actions rather than years."

The coach rolled to a stop in front of the townhouse, located at the end of the long brick terrace. The brick had been covered with a plaster stucco and painted a creamy pale salmon with maritime blue door and trim. To the left of the entrance, a bow window shone with a warm welcoming light and a pair of pilasters on each side of the three steps leading up to the door. Above, miniature wrought-iron balconies graced the windows of the top three stories, which would hold baskets of flower in the summer.

The door opened and a butler appeared with a stiff bow and a bewildered expression. The look was explained as Lady Roberta pushed her ample bulk through the doorway, sending the poor man in a forward spin. Bertie grabbed his arm with her beringed fingers, her brown eyes slanted with merriment, and pulled him from mishap.

"You almost went tumbling down the stairs, Smith! Really, you should be more careful. I don't know what we'd do without you." She floated down the stairs, always a remarkable sight due to her plump figure, and informed the neighborhood that they had arrived. "My lovelies," she said in a booming welcome, "I've been waiting forever and a day! Come give me a hug. It's been monstrous long since I've seen you both."

The attendant opened the door and helped Hannah from the coach. The weak streetlamp cast a golden glimmer on Aunt Bertie's face that made her appear years younger as she met Hannah at the pavement. She grabbed her niece in a tight hug before she could say a word. After an air-sucking welcome, Hannah managed, "Goodness, it is good to see you too, Aunt."

She gave her brother a sidelong glance and saw Nathaniel maintaining a polite expression while preparing himself for the forthcoming attack. Her brother had always been slightly intimidated by their independent aunt. While their father had been cordial and compliant, his sister had been full of life, pushy, and vocal in her opinions.

At seventeen, Lady Roberta had wed a wealthy baronet's second son. The father had wanted to move up in society, and Bertie had wanted his handsome son. *"It may not have been love at first sight, but it was certainly lust at first touch,"* she'd confided to those present on her niece's sixteenth birthday. It was the first time Hannah had seen her mother blush.

Lady Roberta's robust husband, however, had one major flaw. He could not swim. While on a business trip, his ship had encountered a storm and sank. The marriage contract had provided well for the widow, including a substantial jointure until she remarried or died. Finding herself plump in the pocket and independent, she shunned all future marriage proposals. At fifty almost fifty years of age, she was still dogged by a reputation of bold flirtation and speaking her mind.

Hannah adored her Aunt Bertie. Nathaniel remained cautiously affectionate. Their mother secretly envied her.

"You must be famished. I've arranged a light repast in the parlor. I thought it would be cosier than the dining room." Lady Roberta gave orders to the footman and driver, then turned to the butler and maid. Bodies went scurrying in different directions, trunks were hauled inside, and Hannah soon found herself shed of her traveling cape and sipping a steaming cup of tea.

"You look well, Aunt," Hannah said as she filled a small plate with a chunk of cheese, sliced beef, and a thick piece of buttered bread. "And this is delicious."

Nathaniel agreed, his cheeks full as he took another bite of the meat, quickly followed by more cheese. "I didn't realize how hungry I was." He leaned back against the stuffed brocade with a sigh. "My back is stiff from so many hours in the saddle. I shall retire early tonight."

"Thank you, Hannah, I've taken to walking every day. It adds color to my cheeks, and I feel better." Patting her gray-streaked auburn bun, she continued chatting as she bit into chunk of the blue-streaked Stilton. "I've also ordered cream cheese. It's monstrous good on biscuits.

The small hearth had a cheery fire, the coals burning red and orange. On the mantel were cameos of their grandparents, their father, and Roberta. Likenesses from years ago when the entire family had been alive. The Brussels carpet beneath her feet had been there since Hannah could remember. She traced the now-faded red floral medallions that had once brightened the room with her toe, letting memories envelop her. Her grandmother had decorated this space with vivid, warm colors and personal curiosities and portraits. Aunt Bertie refused to change anything in this room, and Hannah was happy for it.

Grandmama had insisted her grandchildren visit annually, and she and Nathaniel had stayed a week each year near St. Nicholas Day. They received gifts, something they might have asked for throughout the course of the year. How Grandmama always knew, they never did find out. Cook would let them into the kitchen and help prepare the mince pies that would be eaten on Christmas Day. Parlor games were played every night before the fire, and an ongoing tale read to them with a special sweet treat before retiring for the night. Visits here, until the death of their grandmother, had been magical and highly anticipated.

Those weeks came to mind when she thought of her own children she would have someday. Children who would know the feel of their mother's arms around them, kisses at bedtime, and a welcome lap when they needed comforting from a fall off their pony or a dispute with a sibling. It would be the late Lady Pendleton that Hanna would emulate when she was a wife and mother.

Mama loved her children, but one would not describe her as warm nor overly affectionate. Yet, she was responsible for Hannah's confidence and fearlessness in making her voice heard. She had instilled a steely graciousness in her daughter that would bide her well against the vicious tongues of the *beau monde*. Hannah had also inherited her mother's sense of fashion and quick wit. If only Hannah knew what her father had passed on to her. Perhaps that would be a conversation with Aunt Bertie during a quiet evening spent at home.

This was one of the few places that held memories of happy family gatherings. She rose and touched the silver frames, her finger trailing along the delicately engraved metal.

"You were stunning, Aunt," she said, stopping at the likeness of Lady Roberta. "Yet you never married again."

"Pshaw! I had no desire to let another man dictate my comings and goings. My widowhood allowed me almost the same freedom as a man. I can't tell you how that irked the ladies of the *ton.* Green with envy, they were." She grinned, the dimple appearing in her left cheek. "All that whispering about my *peculiarities* and unladylike behavior was driven by jealousy. I decided at an early age, if I was to be accused of something, I may as well get some pleasure from my supposed wicked deeds."

"But did you never love anyone again? Enough to want to spend the rest of your life with him?" Hannah couldn't imagine not marrying or having children. Perhaps no one else had compared to her husband. "Or was your husband your true love?"

"He was my first love," she said wistfully, her brown eyes softening. "But not true love. He... I... Well, that's a story for another day."

"He was a handsome man, my brother, wasn't he?" Aunt Bertie changed the subject, picking up another frame. "I still miss him every day. You have his best traits, Nathaniel. The golden-brown hair and tawny eyes, his athletic nature and generosity of spirit."

"And I never knew him." Hannah had heard the stories, of course, and had listened to countless comments from her mother and aunt. Her mother had never been reticent in her disdain for her husband. Her aunt had never believed the rumors of her brother's infidelities. Nathaniel rarely spoke on the subject at all. "I wish I'd had the chance." *To make up my own mind on his character or lack of.*

"He was a good man, regardless of the on-dits at the time," her aunt consoled. "Just not strong enough for this world *or* your mother. A gentle soul who was never meant to shoulder such heavy responsibility. If my eldest brother had survived, *he* would have been perfect for Lady Pendleton. Proper, rigid—"

Nathaniel cleared his throat, indicating his unease with the direction the conversation had taken.

She ignored him and continued speaking to Hannah. "You are at an age now where we should have a long talk about the past. *Before* we attend any public functions."

"For tonight, let us be glad to be together again. What a

splendid season it shall be, eh?" Nathaniel's voice lifted in false enthusiasm, and both women recognized it.

"Lud! Do not fret, nephew, I will not slight your mother," she relented. "Now, how was the trip? Uneventful, I hope."

"I don't think you've ever hoped for that," mumbled Nathaniel.

"Dull. I forgot to bring a book and thought I would go mad." Hannah whispered loudly, "I have taken to novels as of late."

"And with that tidbit of information, I shall take my leave."

She watched her brother depart, then turned her attention to a shelf with glass and ivory figurines. She picked up a tiny china bell and smiled at the clear, light *tinkle*.

"Your father bought that for Mama before he went off to university. I swear that woman kept everything." A thoughtful expression crossed her still lovely face. "She was a sentimental soul. She passed that tenderness on to her son and the good sense to me. Another reason I never married again."

"You don't approve of marriage?"

"Of course I do! Marriage is a wonderful institution for some. I tried it, enjoyed it, and moved on to the next adventure."

"So no regrets?"

"Ah, that's a tricky question. One always has regrets. More to the point, would I do it the same way again?" Aunt Bertie nodded, her dimple deepening. "Without a doubt."

http://aubreywynne.com/book/earl-of-darby/

AUTHOR'S NOTE

I confess, I didn't start this book out intending it to be so research heavy. I'm not sure what possessed me to have a physician and an historian in the same book, but I certainly did enjoy everything I learned while doing it.

Some inventions they had even then really surprised me, like the stethoscope and others were in the infancy stages of beginning, like anesthesia. I put a considerable amount of time into trying to identify exactly what Dr. Bailey could be using in his experimentation and that was how I happened upon the use of carbon dioxide in anesthesia. Henry Hill Hickman was a young surgeon in Ludlow who would utilize carbon dioxide to suffocate a subject until it lost consciousness. At that point, he would perform surgeries to see if there was any pain. Attempts to share his findings and have them seen in a positive light, however, fell short. First with England, then later with France. There's a little more than what I'm sharing here as I know some people can be sensitive to certain details. If you are curious to learn more, please do research Henry Hill Hickman.

He died young and without recognition for what he'd accomplished. However, now he is considered one of the fathers of anesthesia. His experiments began in 1823 and were doubtfully not shared with other surgeons at the time, so I did use some creative liberty in this book in making the experimentation a couple years earlier and through Dr. Bailey.

Penelope's research wasn't the only one that proved fascinating. MacKenzie's historical facts were a blast to look into and I learned so much about Ancient Greece!

I hope you enjoyed reading the research I did in Penelope and MacKenzie's story as much as I enjoyed learning all these historical tid bits to share. And if you're anything like me, I have a newfound appreciation for those who suffer through the pain of gout!

ACKNOWLEDGMENTS

THANK YOU TO my amazing beta readers who helped make this story so much more with their wonderful suggestions: Kacy Stanfield, Janet Barrett, Tracy Emro and Rachael Keefe. You ladies are so amazing and make my books just shine!

Thank you to Janet Kazmirski for the final read-through you always do for me and for catching all the little last minute tweaks.

Thank you to John Somar and my wonderful minions for all the support they give me.

Thank you to Erica Monroe who saves my life time after time for doing an amazing job with edits and is always there for whatever I need. I swear, you add more years back onto my life with all the help and laughter you bring me.

And a huge thank you so much to my readers for always being so fantastically supportive and eager for my next book.

ABOUT THE AUTHOR

Madeline Martin is a USA TODAY Bestselling author of Scottish set historical romance novels filled with twists and turns, adventure, steamy romance, empowered heroines and the men who are strong enough to love them.

She lives a glitter-filled life in Jacksonville, Florida with her two daughters (known collectively as the minions) and a man so wonderful he's been dubbed Mr. Awesome. She loves Disney, Nutella, wine and could easily lose hours watching cat videos.

Find out more about Madeline at her website:

http://www.madelinemartin.com

facebook.com/MadelineMartinAuthor

twitter.com/MadelineMMartin

instagram.com/madelinemmartin

bookbub.com/profile/madeline-martin

ALSO BY MADELINE MARTIN

BORDERLAND LADIES

Marin's Promise

Anice's Bargain

Ella's Desire

Catriona's Secret

Leila's Legacy

BORDERLAND REBELS

Faye's Sacrifice

Clara's Vow

Kinsey's Defiance

Drake's Determination

HIGHLAND PASSIONS

A Ghostly Tale of Forbidden Love

The Madam's Highlander

The Highlander's Untamed Lady

Her Highland Destiny

Highland Passions Box Set Volume 1

REGENCY NOVELLAS AND NOVELS

Earl of Benton

Earl of Oakhurst

Mesmerizing the Marquis

HARLEQUIN HISTORICALS

How to Tempt a Duke (Harlequin Historical)

HEART OF THE HIGHLANDS

Deception of a Highlander
Possession of a Highlander
Enchantment of a Highlander

THE MERCENARY MAIDENS

Highland Spy
Highland Ruse
Highland Wrath